STANLEY MAXWELL

The **Man** Who Couldn't Be Killed

An incredible story of faith and courage during
China's Cultural Revolution

Pacific Press® Publishing Association
Nampa, Idaho
Oshawa, Ontario, Canada
www.pacificpress.com

Edited by Marvin Moore
Designed by Tim Larson
Cover art by Betty Blue
Typeset in 10/12 New Century Schoolbook

Additional copies of this book may be purchased at
http://www.adventistbookcenter.com

Library of Congress Cataloging-in-Publication Data:

Maxwell, Stanley M., 1958-
    The man who couldn't be killed : an incredible story of
faith and courage during China's cultural revolution /
Stanley Maxwell
    p.   cm.

ISBN 13: 978-0-8163-1235-1
ISBN 10: 0-8163-1235-4

    1. Persecution—China. 2. China—History—Cultural
Revolution, 1966-1969 I. Title.
    BR1608.C6M39   1995
    291.1′772′0951—dc20   94-26486
                                             CIP

06 07 08 • 10 9 8 7

CONTENTS

DEDICATION

Dedicated to:
My Grandpa ("Uncle Arthur"),
Mom, Dad ("Uncle Mervyn"),
Phemie, and the "Wong" family.

AUTHOR'S NOTE:

Gentle Reader:

Since the publication of several articles based on "Mr. Wong's" true story, I have received calls and letters from three continents asking for more information about him.

The facts in this book are real, based on numerous pages of primary sources, two trips to China, interviews with the family, photographs, tapes, and the investigation of actual sites. The "Wong" family often rendered entire conversations. While true to detail, the perspectives of different sources naturally varied somewhat.

Source materials were translated as needed from Mandarin to Cantonese to English. Chinese languages lack the tenses of English, which accounts for some discrepancies.

"Mr. Wong" is *not* the man's real name! The real "Mr. Wong" is not Robert Wong, nor is it David Lin. Both of these were Shanghainese who were also jailed for their faith. Robert Wong, who knows "Mr. Wong," personally, asked me to change the name to "Mr. Li," because many readers had asked if he is *The Man Who Couldn't Be Killed.* I tried complying, but my readers objected. So "Mr. Wong" it is.

Many thanks are due those who helped in the writing of this book: Marvin Moore, for challenging me to write it; Drs. Georgina Hill, Bruce Closser, and Kermit Netteberg, for literary advice; Phemie Cheng (my wife), for translating; Dr. C. Mervyn Maxwell (my dad), for proofreading and; a Chinese historian from Nanjing, for historical and cultural advice; and the "Wong" family, for patiently telling and retelling the story.

Stanley Maxwell
Hong Kong
April 15, 1993

Chapter 1

UP THE WHAMPOA INTO THE BUND

THE HAI SHING FERRY rode up the murky Whampoa River toward Shanghai. This, my third trip to the city, was for an upcoming book to interview a Chinese Christian, whom I will call "Mr. Wong," known in China as The Man Who Couldn't Be Killed. The other trips, by train and plane in 1986, had been for pleasure on my spring break from teaching English and culture to college students at YanBian University in Jilin Province in northeastern China, fifty kilometers north of the North Korean border.

The ferry neared the Bund, a harbor so incredibly muddy that berthing large freighters was virtually impossible. With its clock towers, mansions, and grand hotels, the Bund, unchanged even today, resembles more of a Victorian town than a Chinese city. The Bund, part of the British section of Shanghai in the wild days of Western imperialism before the Communist takeover in 1949, was the center of the opium trade, mobsters, drug dealers, prostitutes, and compradors.

I'd come to learn about life in China during World War II and afterward, when Mao Tse-tung, the son of a peasant from Hunan Province, made his Long March and defeated Nationalist (Kuomintang) President Chiang Kai-shek, enabling Mao to become Communist Party chairman and slam shut China's doors.

After the Communist liberation in 1949, the imperialists and foreign missionaries were booted out of the country in the early fifties, and the Bund ceased being British. Many Kuomintang government workers and military staff, capitalists, gangsters, and Chinese Christians couldn't flee to the United States, Hong Kong, or Taiwan, so the Communist government persecuted them. Mr. Wong was one of these. The Communists sent him to a hard labor camp in Tsinghai, a province near Tibet, where he was intermittently tortured for twenty years for his belief in Jesus. I had come to China to learn his story.

After the ferry docked and unloaded, vans transported the passengers to the customs gate. I stood in line until it came my turn to hand my passport to the officials and waited until Phemie Cheng, my translator from Hong Kong, had her passport processed. Then we left the immigration center and walked the gray streets in search of bus 22, which would take us to the home of Mr. Wong.

****

Phemie was too short to reach the top of the door of the apartment house, so she asked me to press the hidden button behind the house number above the door. I did, and the door opened a crack. A woman peeked out. When she saw a "red-headed foreign devil," she quickly shut the door, but Phemie shouted, "Whey!" The woman knew the voice and reopened the door.

Stepping into an entryway, I held onto the bannister as we climbed the dimly lighted three flights of wooden steps. On the third floor, Phemie asked me to reach up to another doorbell. I did, this time on tiptoe. Just as I stepped down, the door swung out, barely missing me. Mr. Wong's middle daughter, "Lin," welcomed us. We climbed two more flights of stairs, walked down a hall, passed two bedrooms, and entered a spacious living room. The place was furnished with a piano, a desk, a pair of crickets chirping at each other from separate cages, two dressers, two beds, stereo equipment, and, on the balcony, a couple of potted grapevines tied to bamboo poles.

In the center of the room, sitting at a table, a white-haired man with slightly rounded shoulders beamed his radiant smile. Smooth except for a few lines on his forehead, his eighty-something face could easily have passed for a man thirty years his junior—a remarkable feat for a Chinese. And Mr. Wong had spent twenty years in a hard labor camp! His alert eyes revealed a delightful twinkle. He chuckled happily when I entered, for he had been expecting me.

I lifted the backpack from my shoulders, unzipped it, and handed out gifts for the family—a necessary tradition in Chinese culture. Lin accepted hers and disappeared into the master bedroom next to the living room.

Phemie and I sat at the table with Mr. Wong and his son-in-law, "Wan Li," who spoke almost perfect English. "We once used this room for house church services every week," Phemie translated for Mr. Wong. "That's why we have a piano for singing hymns. We brought in benches and set them up for the church members, who crowded in all the way into the hallway! I'm an elder for the house church."

He looked over his shoulder to be sure no one was in the room besides us, then leaned forward and said in a low voice, "Don't tell anyone until next week, but this weekend I've been asked to preach at a house church in Wuxi. I don't care if the government cuts off my head, I'm going! Remember," he said as he pressed his finger to his lips, "don't tell my daughter. She might unwittingly tell a judas, who would report to the government. I'm afraid if anyone knows I'm going out of town this weekend, there may be trouble for the house church service in Shanghai. We never know when the government might raid a house church, arrest the leaders, and carry away everything in the home that's not nailed down. If I'm present during the raid, the authorities won't do it. The police know me. I'm a true Christian! Thus, they're more afraid of me than I am of them! They know I follow the Chinese constitution." He reached into his pocket and pulled out a train ticket. "The house church members paid my way. They're hungering to hear my story!"

"May I ask you some questions about your story?" I asked as I dug into my backpack. I pulled out a pocket tape recorder, placed it on the table, and pushed the Record button.

"What questions do you have? I'll tell you anything!" With Phemie at my right and Wan Li at my left, the tape recorder rolled, and Wan Li translated. I scribbled frantically into my notebook as Mr. Wong began to tell his story. . . .

Chapter 2

DREAM OF RED MANSIONS

The tall, round yellow tower stood near the dusty yellow walls of the Japanese section of Shanghai. Here, Glorious Country Wong worked on the police force, guarding the beat around a clothing factory and the living quarters of its workers. From the window, he watched for any suspicious activity on both sides of the walls. Bored by his monotonous job, Mr. Wong looked forward to giving his wife the surprise he had in his pocket.

When his shift ended, he climbed down the circling staircase and hurried through rows of gray brick three-story apartment complexes within the walls of the compound. Passing a Japanese garden in a courtyard, he bounded up three flights of wooden stairs, ducked under clothes hanging on bamboo poles, opened the first door to his right, and entered the hallway, calling, "Lu, I've come already! Where are you?"

"I'm in the kitchen," his wife called.

Lu was squatting on the floor, wringing out laundry. She looked up at him.

"I bought tickets to the opera." Mr. Wong flashed a charming smile, which lighted up his face.

His wife stood up and wrung out a pair of pants. The water rippled through the cloth before falling into the basin. "When's the show?"

"Tonight. Two hours from now!"

She threw him a dirty look as she twisted the pants again, spraying out beads of water, then draped them over the kitchen windowsill. "Tonight? I can't do that. I'm in the middle of doing laundry! Whatever will I wear?"

"Wear whatever you like."

Hurriedly, his wife squeezed out a shirt and laid it with other wet clothes that she carried outside and hung over bamboo poles. Pulling some dry clothes off other bamboo poles, she returned inside and disappeared into their bedroom down the hall. Within moments, she reappeared, dressed and ready to go.

Together, they left the compound and walked through the bustling streets of Shanghai to the opera building. Flanking its seven doorways, posters depicted the singers in that evening's show, *The Dream of Red Mansions*. The story, based on a Chinese classic, glorified the decadent life of the wealthy who lived during the Ch'ing Dynasty before the Nationalist Revolution of 1913 and the rise of Chiang Kai-shek and his Kuomintang Army.

Eager ticket holders shoved against each other trying to be the first through the door. Mr. Wong reached his hand over several heads, hoping his ticket would be taken prior to others. It was.

Once inside, they pressed through the dimly lighted lobby. He escorted his wife down the middle aisle of the opera house to a pair of empty seats near the front, close enough to the stage that the couple could easily distinguish the features of each actress.

The opera began with the twang of a cord, the beat of a drum, and the entrance of a dancer deftly leaping across the stage in rhythm with the music. Her face, painted with an orange, green, and black mask, made her look like a favored princess. Her long, flowing white robe swept the floor. Another actress, not as attractive, joined her. An operatic quarrel ensued between the two, ending with shrill singing. Their wailing notes pierced the ceiling and thrilled the audience.

Mr. Wong didn't hear the music. His mind focused on the princesslike face of the first actress, her round almond eyes and double eyelids, her thick eyebrows and eyelashes, and her lovely white skin. He loved the contours of her figure and her dark brown hair, which fell elegantly onto her shoulders. Her every move was the material of poetry. He wanted her for himself.

But he worried. Was she already married? A beauty like her

probably had any number of suitors.

His mind flashed back to 1927, long before he'd become a police officer. He was almost twenty when he stood under a bridge, contemplating suicide. He'd recently moved to Shanghai from Anhui Province but had been unable to find work. Before he'd left Anhui, his mother had admonished him to bring honor to his ancestors. When a pickpocket in Shanghai stole all his cash, he felt he'd failed the family name. Rather than starve to death, he'd decided to end his life in a watery grave. Lacking the courage to jump, he'd hid in a corner and wept.

Another man camping under the Whampoa River bridge saw him. "Come," the stranger said, "look at this newspaper clipping. You look like a person who'd qualify for this ad for policemen."

"But I've had no experience, and my education is limited," Mr. Wong said. "I'm afraid I'd never pass their rigorous entrance exam."

His new friend pooh-poohed his excuses with, "A man of your height and build is perfect for the police force. Let's apply together!"

Because of his good looks, large physique, and winning personality, Mr. Wong got the job. Later, his outward appearance and inward discipline brought rapid promotions to a rank where he could demand bribes, which made him wealthy.

Reflecting on his past as he sat in the theater, Mr. Wong reasoned that if his personal appearance could land him a police post, this opera singer would be unable to resist him. Unlike his unexpressive countrymen, Mr. Wong knew his face expressed a wide range of emotions. His eyes twinkled, exuding boundless energy, and he could boast an engaging smile. Though most Chinese shied away from talking to strangers unless first spoken to, he delighted in striking up conversations with people he didn't know. Besides, he could attend the opera, a privilege only the rich could enjoy in freewheeling Shanghai. He also knew that entertainers felt inadequate and needed patrons, for people looked down on them as slaves. A proposal of marriage from him could provide the security she desired. Surely, this packet of assets would prove irresistible to this new idol on the stage!

Then he remembered his wife. Though timid and soft-spoken, she, too, was attractive. With her round face, high-set Oriental eyes, and faint eye line, her features contrasted with the charming opera singer. Mr. Wong loved his wife and was proud to be her husband. He tipped his head so he could speak into her ear. "Lu, I think the singer is very pretty. What do you think?"

"Which one?"

"The one in white," Mr. Wong replied, his eyes riveted on the actress's face.

"Yes, she's pretty."

Always quick acting and blunt, he whispered, "I think I want her for my second wife. Do you object?"

Silence. Lu wanted to keep him for herself, but she whispered, "No, I don't mind—if she'll keep your eyes from looking at other women."

Mr. Wong smiled, thinking his wife was very generous. She loved him deeply and only desired his happiness. Women are superior judges of character. In concern for her happiness, he proposed, "We don't know what this woman's like; she may be difficult for you to live with. If you like her, she'll be all right. Why don't I rent a hotel room in Suzhou for a few weeks? You two can live together without me. Afterward, tell me how you get along. If you fight a lot, then I won't marry her, but if you like each other, I will."

"That's good," his wife agreed.

Mr. Wong paid no attention to the opera, thinking only of the singer in white. When the show ended, he pressed through the crowd, strode confidently up the steps of the stage, and ushered himself backstage, where he peeped into a few dressing rooms until he saw the pretty actress before a mirror rubbing off her makeup.

"How are you?" He beamed. "I'm Glorious Country Wong, and I think you're the most beautiful woman in the opera. So does my wife."

"Thank you," she replied. "I'm Soong. What can I do for you?"

Mr. Wong shot straight to the point. "I want you to be my second wife."

"Married to a handsome gentleman like you—" She looked

Mr. Wong up and down, trying to read his character. Charmed by his clean white suit and muscular build, her eyes glowed with a combination of Chinese dollar signs and love at first sight. Without hesitation, she answered, "All right, I agree!"

Elated, his eyes sparkled as a flurry of words followed. "I'll rent a hotel room in Suzhou for three weeks. You can live there with my wife. I think you should know what you're getting into before we get married, so you need time to get acquainted with her. I don't want you two squabbling and miserable. After three weeks, if you become like sisters, I'll take you as my second wife. If you don't like each other, the marriage is off. Either one can call it off. My wife has agreed to this arrangement."

"You're very kind, Glorious Country Wong," Soong answered. "Your plan is good."

"I'll tell my wife. Then we'll get a room for you." With that, Mr. Wong returned to his wife, sure that she would like Soong— and that his life would never be the same again.

Chapter 3

TWO BIBLES IN THE LOOT

In 1937, the streets of Shanghai, usually bustling, were eerily empty, almost dead. Though the shops were open, no one, not even the owners, were inside. Not a hawker squatted on the tile sidewalks. No beggars sat with outstretched hands. Gone were the bony coolies balancing heavy loads. Even the rickshaw drivers and the chauffeur-driven black sedans had vanished. The stillness spelled suspense and danger.

World War II was in full swing. Cross-fire from Japanese occupation forces and Chinese snipers from the resistance had made Shanghai's streets a battlefield. Mr. Wong, who'd quit his police job to lead a squadron that sniped against the Japanese, patrolled the streets around the Japanese section. Most residents had fled, leaving their belongings behind.

Exploring the area cautiously, with his gun ready, he listened intently. Stepping into a pharmacy, he found it stocked with traditional Chinese medicine. Dried herbs and jars of preserved marine animals lined the walls. Ginseng, boxes of royal jelly, and bottles of pills were stacked on the floor.

Two black books with golden edges caught his attention. Curious, he picked one up and read "The Old and New Testaments." That meant nothing to him. He leafed through the pages, amazed at how thin they were—perfect for rolling cigarettes. His Number One Wife, Lu, could use them, for paper was scarce in wartime.

A noise startled him. He grabbed the books, tucked them inside his jacket, and crouched behind the counter. Peeping out, he saw nothing unusual. Yet a good sniper wasn't easily detected. *Why not go home?* he thought. *At least it's comfortable, and no place is safe.* He'd rather face danger in a familiar place than in the pharmacy.

Standing up, he headed for the door, picking up a bottle of medicine as he left. Out on the deserted street he saw several snipers, like himself, dash out of a store carrying armloads of loot. He smiled, knowing he wasn't the only one pillaging.

Passing the familiar yellow walls of his compound, he came to the apartment complex that housed his two wives. He ran up the wooden stairs, eager to show Lu his surprise.

"Whey, Lu!" he called.

"Whey!" she answered.

He stepped down from the hall into the kitchen and found Lu steaming rice. "I've got something for you."

"What is it?"

He drew the books from under his jacket. "Look."

"Books! Golden edges! That's nice." His wife began dicing vegetables and meat. "What's the title?"

"Old and New Testaments."

"Aiya!" she exclaimed. "That's the Christian book of the foreign devils! The wicked Western imperialists use it to help dominate our poor nation. It's filled with useless superstition. Are you sure you want to read that?"

Mr. Wong laughed. "No, you don't understand. You don't need to read the book, nor do I."

She poured oil in a wok and tossed in a handful of diced meat. "What do you want with a Christian book if you're not planning to read it and be a Christian?"

"Look at the paper, Lu!" Mr. Wong opened a book. "Fine quality. Perfect for you!"

"For me?" She dumped diced vegetables into her wok, stirring them into the sizzling meat.

"Yes, you can use this paper for making shoe patterns."

His wife smiled. "Old Husband has good ideas in his head. Here I thought you wanted to become a Christian. Paper for shoe patterns costs a lot of money these days. I'll put the books under the bed."

Weeks passed. The Japanese left Shanghai, and Mr. Wong got a job as supervisor policing the area around the WahTung Garment Factory. Answering the door one day, Lu welcomed Ma Lizhi, one of the textile workers at the factory, who'd stopped to visit.

"May I have a shoe pattern?" he asked.

"Come," she said, and he followed her into the main room. The room had a tatami mat on the floor and a paper-thin wall with a sliding door dividing the children's sleeping quarters from that of the parents. In the corner her son Lee and daughter Mei-Mei played near a large wooden bed. Lu reached under it, pulled out one of the Testaments with the golden edges, and tore out two pages. She knelt down and placed the paper on the floor. "Stand on this, please."

He obeyed. "Where'd you get the paper?"

"Old Husband brought it home. He found two books with golden edges and gave them to me." Lu traced his foot on the paper. "Lift up. Now put your other foot here." She pointed to the other page on the floor.

As she worked, he picked up the book and thumbed through it. "Says Old and New Testament. Do Christians tear their holy books?"

"Aiya! We're not Christian," Lu snapped. "I wouldn't believe that foreign-devil religion. We have the book only because I need paper. Due to war, paper's too expensive."

The customer examined the texture of the pages. "This paper's very good."

"You're right! Excellent paper. Best for making shoe patterns. Can you rip out another page and hand it to me?"

The door in the hall opened. Lu knew her husband had arrived. "Soong!" he called, and Lu saw his look of disappointment when he saw her.

"Lu, is Soong here?" Lu continued molding her shoe pattern into a paper sandal. She detected a storm brewing. Possibly silence would divert an argument.

Ever since that night at the opera when her husband had fallen for the opera singer, things hadn't been the same. In the hotel she and Soong had eaten together, shared the same bed, told each other their favorite stories, and become fast friends. Soong—Lu called her "Little Sister"—was beautiful from her skin to her heart. After the marriage, Soong had kept her husband from chasing other women, as Lu had hoped. Though Soong was his Favorite Wife, Lu had the status of First Wife and had gained Soong as a mutual confidant, something her husband had never been. In many ways, life had improved.

When Soong entered the family, her singing had brought increased wealth. Consequently, their husband had become preoccupied with a new vice—gambling. But with Soong expecting a baby, the number of her performances was destined to decrease and her cash flow to dwindle.

Lu dawdled on the shoe pattern, dreading to be left alone with her husband in his present mood. She looked up. His polite smile appeared ready to drop to the floor.

"Where's Soong?" Her husband fidgeted nervously in his shirt pocket for his cigarettes.

"Little Sister Soong sings nights and sleeps days when she's not rehearsing."

"I know! I know!" He sounded on the verge of exasperation.

"Why don't you go to the opera house?" She heard him open the door and descend the stairs. He'd return, but until then she'd have peace.

She put the final touches on the shoe pattern and handed it to her customer. "Is this good or not?"

He looked it over and approved.

"I'll get started on your shoes right away," Lu said as she escorted him down the hall.

Her husband reentered. "When's Soong coming back?"

"When the rehearsal's over." Lu cut cloth to make the sandal. "Anything I can do?"

"No, no! I need Soong. You don't hold the purse strings."

"How much money do you want this time?" Lu started sewing the shoes. "Were you playing mahjongg?"

"I don't gamble at mahjongg," her husband snapped. "I'm not good enough. I'm a champion Chinese chess player. No one can beat me at chess!"

Lu wondered why he needed money. After a moment, she ventured, "The end of the road for gamblers is a lonely place filled with nothing but poverty."

"I'm a policeman married to a wealthy second wife. I need money for my status." He lighted another cigarette. "Poverty will never knock at my door. If I'm desperate for money, I'll demand higher bribes."

Lu detested his arrogant pride. She poked the needle into the shoe and pulled the thread along. "Just because you're a policeman doesn't mean you're above the law."

"Aiya, woman, mind your insolence! I won't be *cho*!" When her husband trumpeted *cho*, he meant henpecked outcast. "I know what I'm doing!" he yelled. "If I want your advice, I'll ask for it."

Knowing she'd said too much already, she sewed the shoes in silence, hoping her comments would germinate from seeds of thought into ideas of his own.

"Where's Soong anyway?" Her husband interrupted Lu's reverie. "She should be home by now."

"She'll come."

"Whatever's she doing?"

"Probably walking home. Why don't you go meet her?"

"Because I'm here now, and she should be here too." Just then, the door opened, and Soong pattered toward the living room.

Mr. Wong smiled affectionately. "It's Soong. Soong's here."

He almost jumped up and down like a schoolboy. Lu felt hurt. Soong was obviously his favorite, for they never quarreled about anything. Soong seldom disagreed with him. Would she grant his wish for money? Lu hoped against feeble hope that Soong would say No.

"What were you two arguing about? Did it have something to do with me?"

"What makes you think we were quarreling?" Mr. Wong feigned an air of innocence.

"I heard your voices three floors down," Soong said as she walked to the bed and lay down.

"Yes, we were talking about you," Lu admitted.

"What's the fight about?"

"He lost gambling."

"I didn't lose a game. No one beats me at Chinese chess." Mr. Wong lighted another cigarette.

"The only time you want money," Lu bantered, "is when you lose a game!"

"I never lose!" Mr. Wong blew smoke in Lu's direction.

Lu wondered why she even tried to help her husband give up gambling. Soong seemed to think that because money came easily, it should be spent freely. Didn't she know that as her belly grew, her time on stage would shrink? Lu wondered how Soong would adjust when money became tight or when her pretty face faded and she could no longer sing opera. "If you didn't lose, why do you always want money?"

"Excuse me!" Soong tried to outshout the other two. "I don't understand. What's the problem? Where do I come in?"

Lu and her husband regained their composure.

"I need money for a party I threw last night. Will you give me some, Soong?"

Lu laughed cynically; then silence hung menacingly over the room. Money for a party, not for food and drink, but for betting money with mahjongg blocks. No doubt he'd lost the wagers and needed money to save face for his reputation so he could play and lose again gracefully. Lu prayed to all the gods that Soong would refuse, for such humiliation might help him break his addiction to gambling. Her heart beat rapidly as she awaited Soong's decision.

"I have a concert to worry about, and I'm tired." Soong let her long brown hair fall to her shoulders. "I'll give you what you want just to get peace and quiet. How much do you need?"

Lu felt sick again.

Mr. Ma Lizhi walked past the rows of black sewing machines, with workers bowed before them pushing cloth to the hungry needle. He'd finished his workday at the clothing factory and was on his way to Mr. Wong's house to pick up his new cloth shoes.

Near the factory, he saw a large sign hanging from a red brick building advertising "Long-Distance Study." Curious, he stepped inside but found nobody there. Going down a long hall, he found a wall of closed doors. Suddenly, before he could knock, a door opened and a receptionist greeted him. She opened another door, led him into a classroom, and introduced him to an American missionary woman sitting behind a table. Speaking perfect Chinese, the American smiled. "Welcome to the Seventh-day Adventist church."

Slightly flustered, Ma Lizhi said, "I'd like to know about your long-distance study. What would I learn?"

"We have fourteen courses that help you learn about the Old and New Testaments."

"How do I take the courses?"

The woman showed him a sample lesson. "We send you this material, you read it, answer the questions, and mail it back to us. After we've graded it, we send you the next lesson, and the whole process repeats itself. Have any questions?"

"No."

"Would you like to sign up for the long-distance study?" The woman held out a pen for him.

Ma Lizhi didn't want to study, for he was in a hurry to see his shoes. But he remembered the Scriptures with golden edges Lu had grabbed from under her bed. An idea struck him that those Testaments ought to be studied. Thinking the price would be high, he asked, "How much?"

"It's absolutely free." The woman smiled. "Interested?"

"Sure, why not? If it doesn't cost anything." But he had no intention of taking the course himself. Ma Lizhi took the pen and application form from the woman and filled out Glorious Country Wong's name and address. It was the perfect prank.

Outside, as he headed down the street to pick up his new shoes, he chuckled to himself. What would Mr. Wong think when he started receiving a Bible-correspondence course in the mail?

Chapter 4

LONG-DISTANCE STUDY

Mr. Wong awoke early and slipped out of bed, trying not to disturb his Number One Wife Lu. Opening the mahogany trunk beside the bed, he pulled out clean pants, a shirt, and a couple of incense sticks. He lighted them and carried them to the family shrine donated by his Number Two Wife Soong.

The shrine consisted of two shelves. On the upper shelf stood three traditional heroes cast of colorfully hand-painted ceramic: Mr. Prosperity, Mr. Happiness, and Mr. Longevity. Inside a mini Buddhist temple, on the shelf below the three figurines, rested ceramic bowls holding sticks of incense that the family kept burning.

Five books, considered Confucian classics, sat on a low table in front. In these books Confucius describes how all good Chinese should behave.

Mr. Wong faced the shrine, placed his hands together, and meditated until he could no longer hear the rhythmic breathing of his sleeping wife behind him. When he came out of his trance, he knocked the ashes from some incense sticks and knelt on the pillow on the floor in front of the shrine. He waved the sticks up and down, then with cupped hands tried to pull the smoke over his hair and body. Bowing again before the shrine, he placed the sticks with the others burning in the bowls. Picking up Confucius's *Analects*, he began to read. Suddenly Lu's voice interrupted his thoughts.

"There's some mail for you." Lu spoke quietly so as not to awaken Soong and the girls slumbering on the other side of the paper-thin walls that divided their bedrooms.

"Who's it from?" Mr. Wong whispered.

"No one important. Says 'Long-Distance Study' on the envelope."

"Let's see it."

Lu got on all fours, reached under the bed, pulled out a crumpled envelope, and handed it to Mr. Wong.

"The return address is the Seventh-day Adventist church near the factory." He tore it open and scanned the contents.

"What is it?"

"A Bible lesson. I wonder how they got my address."

"Shall I throw it away for you? You don't want to study the Bible, do you?"

"Where are those Bibles I gave you for making shoe patterns?"

"I don't know." Lu laughed. "I haven't made any paper shoe samples for a while."

"Maybe they're under the bed." He bent down, but Lu was on the floor searching for the Bibles before he could reach under the bed. She pulled one out and handed it to him. He placed the letter between its pages.

"Please sit here beside me," Lu invited as she sat on the edge of the bed. Looking into his eyes, she pouted. "There are many things for you to consider, Old Husband. What'll our ancestors think? How'll they eat? Where'll they stay when their houses decay from neglect? They'll be a laughingstock in heaven. Do you want the angry gods sending misfortune on us? Aiya! Do you really think it's safe to study this course?"

Mr. Wong smiled at his superstitious wife. He, too, feared the wrath of the gods if he ignored the ancestors. "You worry too much, Lu. There's no harm in studying the Bible. I'll search for truth and weed out falsehood. I won't do anything foolish."

"Well, I guess you know what's best."

Soong slid the door open and waddled into the room, her belly swollen. Because of her pregnancy, she hadn't performed for months. Soong grumbled good-naturedly, "You woke me up. What's going on?"

"Lu gave me my mail and helped me find one of the Bibles I gave her."

"Ai, what's it all about?" Soong pulled a comb from her robe and dragged it through her hair. As she straightened the snags, she transformed herself in Mr. Wong's mind into the beauty he'd fallen in love with at the opera.

"Old Husband plans to study the Bible with golden edges. Little Sister, what'll happen to the ancestors?" Lu asked.

"Old Husband can do whatever he wants," Soong murmured sleepily. "I'm going back to bed." Mr. Wong smiled at her as she left. Reacting to Lu's objections, he immediately leaned against the wall, opened the letter with the long-distance course, and began reading the questions. With some difficulty, he found the answers in Scripture and wrote them on the answer sheet. That very day he mailed the completed lesson and began waiting for the next.

As Mr. Wong studied, he gained many new ideas. First, he learned about a loving God who sent His only Son to die for sinners so that anyone who believed in Him and claimed His promises could become changed. Jesus wanted to be his Best Friend and to plead for him before God on the basis of His crucifixion so that he needn't die. Through this friendship, God would enable him to put away his sordid past and ultimately strengthen him to do what he couldn't do—obey the Ten Regulations in Exodus 20.

He discovered signs that the world would soon end, but Jesus would come to live with His friends forever. A special group, the remnant, who followed the truth, would be persecuted by the world because they kept the faith of Jesus and the Ten Regulations.

He memorized the First Regulation: "You will have no other Gods before Me." The Second Regulation talked about carved images. Out of the corner of his eye he saw the Buddhist shrine, and a conflict raged within. He remembered what Lu had said about studying the Bible, disregarding his ancestors, and bad luck. Were the ancestors gods, or, in honoring them, was he fulfilling the Fifth Regulation about honoring parents to enjoy a long life? Was he respecting the ancestors or worshiping them? What about the three heroes: Longevity, Prosperity, and Happiness? He mulled over these thoughts.

He memorized the Fourth Regulation. Should his entire household set aside the regular work routine on the seventh-day Sabbath and celebrate holiness? Should he rest from sundown on the sixth day until sundown on the seventh day? He wrestled with the thoughts as he performed guard duty.

The Seventh Regulation caused him extreme worry. How could he, with two wives, resolve adultery and polygamy? The Abram and Hagar story fascinated him. Soong would soon bear him a child. What if it were a son? He could understand disposing of a daughter, for girls married and joined the husband's family, neither carrying on the family name nor looking after their parents in old age. But no Chinese would consider banishing a firstborn son like Ishmael, who would be responsible for his old father's care.

He learned that God wanted him to control both his mouth and his temper. Following Chinese tradition, he used friends to act as middlemen in disputes. But what about his frequent arguments with Lu concerning his passion for Chinese chess and gambling? As a policeman, he'd beaten suspects into confessing their crimes, a standard procedure under the law. Also, out of rage at the Japanese occupation, he'd become a sniper and fought enemies who were his neighbors. Violence, he noted, wasn't heaven's way. Yet Jesus promised that a Christian would take up a sword to fight the dragon.

Dragons fascinated Mr. Wong, since to Chinese they are good and a national mascot. But Revelation 12:17 described an evil dragon cast out of heaven for insurrection. Angrily chasing an earthly woman, it made war against her Child, Christ. When the Child escaped to heaven, the dragon chased the woman and the rest of her offspring, His followers, who obey the Ten Regulations and witness to others about God's Son. Earth was a battle between good and evil. Those who clamored after the dragon were sure losers. Mr. Wong wanted no part in that number, but his life seemed more like the dragon's than the Child's.

He thrilled at the good news that God's Son, the Creator of everything, was faithful and just and would forgive him, if he asked (see 1 John 1:9). The Ten Regulations showed room for improvement that, with the help of his newfound Friend, he could accomplish. Regretting his misdeeds, he longed for eternal life. However, being a Christian meant more than believing—devils believe (see James 2:19). It meant action and a new lifestyle.

Mr. Wong began speaking kindly to Lu. Did she notice? Granted, no Chinese would comment if she had.

Whenever he saw Lu or Soong at the shrine to the ancestors placing "hell bank notes," paper houses, and paper furniture in a tin and setting fire to them, he felt inner conflict between the Second and Fifth Regulations. His Bible told him that the living know that they will die, but the dead know nothing (see Ecclesiastes 9:5) until the second coming and the resurrection. If his ancestors had no life now, his wives needn't burn paper money, paper houses, paper cars, paper furniture, and paper clothes for his ancestors to use in heaven. Dead ancestors don't need anything, because their breath vanishes into the atmosphere.

The time had come for commitment. He must choose between the ancestors and the God of the Old and New Testaments.

Alone, on his knees, Mr. Wong prayed, "Jesus, my Friend, I'm determined to believe You and Your Word. Change my character. Make me refined steel, able to face any test, even pain and disaster. The earth means nothing to me anymore. The Bible says those who don't believe in You will vanish someday like the animals. I choose heaven and long to become Your missionary here and now, ready to sacrifice myself for You, my Friend and Saviour, Jesus, who died for me."

Choosing between God and the ancestors suddenly became easy: the ancestors had to go.

When Lu was shopping one day, Mr. Wong tore down the shrine, threw out the bowl of incense, and buried the three heroes in the trunk. Just as he was shutting the trunk, Soong slid open the door on the paper wall, shuffled into the room holding her swollen belly, and saw the bare wall. "Old Husband! Maybe a thief came into our house."

He guessed she knew everything and had seen his action through the paper wall like a shadow drama. "I took down the shrine because I've learned our ancestors don't need it."

"How can they live without our gifts and generosity?" Soong sat wearily on the trunk to take the weight off her legs.

"We need give nothing to the ancestors because they're asleep," Mr. Wong explained.

"Aiya!" Soong looked at Mr. Wong incredulously. "Then they need a bed to sleep on. We must burn a paper bed for them."

Mr. Wong turned to Genesis 3:19. "When people die, their bodies turn to dust, so they don't need beds." He flipped to the Second Regulation and read it to Soong. "I've decided to be a Christian. I put your three heroes in the trunk. Next time you visit your parents, please take them with you."

Chapter 5

BIGAMY AND BAPTISM

Soong gave birth to a beautiful baby girl in 1946, a week before Mr. Wong graduated from his long-distance Bible course. Whenever the baby cried or cooed, he felt proud to have gained another child, even a girl. Now the forty-year-old father had six mouths to feed—his own, two wives, and their three children.

But his long-distance study troubled him. Pastor Charlie Chu, who'd graded the courses, told him marriage was important to the church. If he wished to be baptized, he must be the husband of only one wife. Polygamy was forbidden. He had to choose between bigamy and baptism. He pleaded with his Friend Jesus to help him solve all his problems.

He stepped into the room where Soong sat on her bed, nursing her bundle of joy. His favorite wife looked so beautiful. He couldn't divorce her. But he couldn't divorce Lu either, for she was his real wife. Following Chinese custom, he could take a second, third, or fourth wife (as many as he could afford), but he must keep the first one. Divorce disgraced a woman, making her into a "ghost"—a pariah worse than a nonperson. How could he do the right thing—not according to culture, but in God's sight—and be baptized?

He sat on the bed. For a moment, as a smiling Soong rocked her baby, Mr. Wong forgot his troubles. The infant made the two adults one, and they both knew it. They basked in each other's company. He couldn't imagine life without her. There had to be another way. Then an idea struck him.

"Soong," he broke the charmed silence, "I want to change our relationship." Soong continued cuddling the baby. "I think we should become like brother and sister."

"I bore your child, Old Husband," Soong retorted. "How can I be your sister?"

"Soong, I've decided to be a Christian." Mr. Wong flashed a smile. "A true Christian can be the husband of only one wife if he wants to be baptized."

"Aiya! You should've considered that before you married me, Old Husband. I'm your Number Two Wife." She rocked the baby more rapidly. "I cannot become your sister. What do we do with the child?"

Mr. Wong arose, walked to the thin sliding door that divided the bedrooms, slid it open, and left Soong alone with the baby. He felt disappointed that she hadn't allowed him to change their relationship to brother and sister, which would be an easy way out. Solving the problem now would be much more difficult. He lacked the courage to press the issue. Through the paper-thin wall, he could see Soong silhouetted on her bed, still rocking the child. His deep love for them both made him ache all the more, knowing what he had to do.

Divorce. He couldn't bring the word to his lips. To pull it off, he'd need a heart of stone. He resisted the thought. Wearily, he lay back on his bed and slept fitfully.

When he awoke, Lu lay asleep beside him. The baby's crying and Soong's stirring had aroused him. He left Lu and entered Soong's room in time to see her commence breast-feeding. She was a good wife and mother. His heart opened to her, but he sealed it tightly.

Sliding the door shut quietly so as not to awaken Mei-Mei sleeping at the other end of the room, he sat beside Soong. Speaking softly, he forced the dreaded words out: "I want a divorce."

"I disagree." She adjusted the baby. "When you met me in the theater, you told me you had another wife, and I agreed to marry you. Your wife agreed. I plan to keep my status."

Mr. Wong, touched by her devotion, wanted to drop the subject, but he had to persist. He spoke again, more insistently. "Soong, I'm not the same man you married. I've learned the truth about God's Ten Regulations. When I married you, I was living in sin. But I've put that behind me now."

"What've I done wrong? I'm innocent." Soong looked her husband in the eye. "Aiya! Please don't disgrace me because you think you made a mistake. What's done is done."

"You're right." He smiled, hoping Soong would understand. "I sinned when I married you. Now I must correct that sin. That's why I must ask for a divorce."

"Aiya, Old Husband, I won't allow you to divorce me." The infant stopped sucking. Soong laid it down.

Mei-Mei rolled over in her bed. If he talked any longer, Mr. Wong feared he might awaken his daughter. In any case, he wasn't persuading Soong, so he stood to leave. "Think about it."

"This is my home," she said firmly as she cradled the sleeping baby in her arms. "Look at our baby. Isn't she beautiful?" She lifted the baby's face toward Mr. Wong. "What'll happen to her if I leave, disgraced? Nobody wants a former Number Two Wife. I'd make a terrible ghost. No, Old Husband, I'm staying."

Righting a wrong is like battling upstream. Everything Soong said was true. His sin would cost him—and her—dearly.

He went to where Lu slumbered, opened the family trunk, and searched for what gold and jewelry he could see in the moonlight. Soong, an opera singer in demand in both Suzhou and Shanghai, could earn money easily for many more years. But, because his sin involved another person, it would cost him and the family financially as well as emotionally.

With his hands full of jewelry and more than ten teals of gold, Mr. Wong returned to where Soong lay with the baby. "It's my duty to provide for your future," he said as he lay the valuables on Soong's bed. "Take these in restitution."

"Do you think my heart's for rent?" Soong sounded insulted. "I'm not a streetwalker you can pick up and pay and she'll go away. I married you because you asked me and your wife agreed. I remain your faithful Number Two Wife." Leaving his gift on Soong's bed, Mr. Wong went back to the family trunk and dug out rings, necklaces, pearls, gemstones, and ten thousand Chinese dollars. He returned to Soong's and Mei-Mei's room with an armload and added it to the pile beside Soong. "I give you all my savings." To give Soong a future, Mr. Wong threw away his own—and that of the rest of his family—certain that his new Friend Jesus would provide his daily rice and water. "Take these too, Soong. We must divorce."

She still refused.

Police duty beckoned. There was no way he could resolve the issue quickly. Sliding the door behind him, he dressed, walked down the corridor, and descended the three flights of steps.

After an uneventful shift at the tower, Mr. Wong bought a *Suzhou Daily News* and retraced his steps to the Japanese compound and home. He thumbed through the newspaper, looking for an advertisement he wanted to show Soong. Though she wouldn't like it, he wanted her to read it anyway. He marked it and took the newspaper to Soong's room, but she was at the opera, and Lu rocked Soong's baby.

He read the news until dusk, then switched on the light, picked up his Testaments, and reviewed a story he planned to tell Soong. When she walked through the door wearing a long, flowing red *cheongsam*, worn traditionally by princesses in the Ch'ing Dynasty, it seemed as if magic had flowed into the room. Mr. Wong rested his eyes lovingly on her face. Soong was a temptation, but he fought to maintain a hard heart.

"Did you wait up for me?" She smiled.

"I must tell you a story and show you something in the newspaper."

"What've you got for me?"

"Please, sit down and listen." Mr. Wong gave her a warm smile. Oh, he wished she could stay. Lu put Mei-Mei to bed, excused herself, then slid the door shut behind her. Soong sat on the bed, gazing adoringly into his commanding eyes. "What's your story?"

"You know I've been studying this book." Mr. Wong indicated his Bible. "After reading it, I've become a new man."

"You spend more time with the children."

"I must become a good father."

"Lu and I decided that you've become a very nice man." Mr. Wong knew she meant he'd quit gambling and quarreling with his wives over money.

"If I'm a good man, it's because of my new Friend, Jesus. After reading about Him in this book, I've decided to follow Him and live a Christian life. Any goodness in me now is a gift from the Real God in heaven."

Soong changed the subject. "You were going to tell me a story, Old Husband."

"My story's about a wealthy man named Abram who had two wives," Mr. Wong began. "His Number One Wife Sarai couldn't bear children, so she asked Abram to marry her servant Hagar and let her give birth to his child. Abram and Sarai loved each other very much, but he needed a son. So Abram took Hagar to be his Number Two Wife. Later, Abram had a son from each wife. Hagar bore him Ishmael, and Sarai gave him Isaac. Ishmael became jealous of Isaac, and God was displeased. He wanted Abram to be husband only to his Number One Wife Sarai. One day the voice of God told Abram to send Hagar and Ishmael away."

"What did Abram do?" Soong was caught up in the story.

"He obeyed the voice of the Real God."

The baby cried out, and Soong picked her up. "Did he send his Number Two Wife and his Number One Son away?"

"Yes."

Soong wrinkled up her nose with worry as she rocked her baby. "What happened to them?"

"They fled into the wilderness, where God provided for their needs. But that's another story."

"Why did he send her away?"

"Abram had displeased the Real God by taking a Number Two Wife. Hagar wasn't really his wife." Mr. Wong looked intently into Soong's eyes as he explained, hoping that she understood the analogy. "Only Sarai was his wife. Polygamy's against God's original plan. He wants a man to have only one wife."

"How can we save face?" She really meant that if he planned to disgrace his favorite wife, the problem was his, not hers.

It pained Mr. Wong to lose the woman he loved. "I want to do what's right." Opening the newspaper, he turned to the marked page and pointed to the spot. "Read this."

Soong read, and a tear rolled down her cheeks, sending a

streak through her pearly white and rosy makeup.

"I announced our divorce in the newspaper, so it's final. I wanted you to become my sister. We could've saved face then, but you refused. I want you in my household, but in God's sight you're not really my wife." Mr. Wong's voice broke. "If I continue living with you as husband and Number Two Wife, I'm living in sin!" Moisture clouded his vision. "I want to take care of you, Soong."

"I'm an opera singer. I have money, so I can take care of myself." Soong really meant she needed nothing but her husband. "Don't worry about me and the baby."

"Our story's different from Abram and Hagar. He sent her away into the wilderness with nothing." Mr. Wong placed his arm around Soong. "I've given you all the family wealth and jewelry, hoping it'll provide for your future."

"You're kind," Soong answered. "How can you ever provide for the rest of your family?"

"God will provide. I'm a Christian now. Jesus is my new Friend and my Saviour. The Bible says that when He created humans, He designed monogamy. I want to follow those teachings." Words didn't come easily. "When I married you, I made a mistake in ignorance that I must now correct."

"What do you want me to do?"

With mixed emotions, he knew Soong was, at last, going to agree to the divorce. "We have a house in Suzhou—it belongs to you and your baby. Lu and the other children will stay in Shanghai and live here with me." He wiped tears that spilled down his cheek, past his chin, and down his neck. "You don't have to go to your parents in disgrace."

Mei-Mei lay awake on her bed, listening to night sounds. She heard her father rustling the pages of the newspaper and her Number Two Mother talking with him. She tried to understand, but many words were beyond her understanding.

She grew curious when she heard footsteps pass her bed and grow quieter down the corridor. Carefully, so as not to wake up her Number One Mother in the next room, Mei-Mei inched off her bed. When she was sure her Number One Mother hadn't stirred, she took a few steps to the door and entered the hall, leaving the door ajar.

She felt cold air. The front door must be open. Moonbeams silhouetted Soong with her baby strapped to her back and her father standing on the balcony. They embraced, and Mei-Mei could hear them talking softly.

Sneaking through the dark, she felt her way with her hand. Safely hidden within the shadows, she crept to within five steps of the door, where she could eavesdrop.

Though she couldn't catch every word, she heard goodbyes and something about a train ticket. Her Number Two Mother pushed away from her father abruptly and said, "I go!" Soong's silhouette stooped to pick up something like a bag, stepped downward and stopped, exposing an elegant profile in the moonlight. The shadow threw back a lock of hair from its reflection. "Don't worry about me."

More goodbyes, then the profile transformed itself into the back of a head, which vanished into the night.

Mei-Mei crept back into her bed before her father entered the corridor. As she heard him slip into his bed, she pondered the empty bed against the wall where Soong had slept. Mei-Mei sensed that the moonlit silhouettes on the balcony would be her last memories of her Number Two Mother and of her tiny half sister.

Lying in bed, Mr. Wong consoled himself that Soong's opera singing would be in demand in Suzhou. Because Chinese considered entertainers slightly crazy, they were tolerant of their behavior. A woman as beautiful as she could find another patron. But the memory of Soong's eyes haunted him. At the first goodbyes, her hazel eyes were loving, but when she'd turned on the steps, she'd flashed a look of hate. As she descended toward the courtyard, he lost a beautiful companion, a lovely child, and most of the family wealth, including their summer house in Suzhou. He'd gladly given his material possessions for Soong's future, for he'd sinned in a relationship that was entirely his fault.

The experience pained him deeply, for he loved and respected her, yet as he dozed off he felt a new peace of mind. Many would consider his actions cruel, but he knew he'd sent her away with dignity. By righting a wrong, he'd climbed another rung on the Christian ladder.

The next morning, when his Number One Wife Lu, who disliked Christianity, learned what he'd done, she exclaimed, "What you did was not by human powers. This is the power of your Real God!" Mr. Wong smiled to himself. Maybe she'd become a Christian too.

Soon he could be baptized and start anew. But first he needed more faith from his newfound Friend, for on the path of faith he foresaw more struggles ahead.

Chapter 6

RESIGNATION

Striding into the police station, Mr. Wong's mind raced with the challenge ahead of him. As he walked, he prayed to his new Friend: "You know I'm living in conflict with both the Fourth and the Eighth Regulations. Help me to do the right thing regardless of the pain. Show me how to care for my family, for we have so little since Soong left."

Since he'd quit smoking, the blue haze of tobacco smoke stung Mr. Wong's eyes. He sat on an armchair facing the desk of his rotund superior. While he awaited recognition, he filled a mug with hot oolong tea from a pitcher on a small glass-covered table.

Finally his boss turned to the last page of his newspaper, looked through his horn-rimmed spectacles, and said, "How are you, Old Wong?"

"Good! How are you?" Mr. Wong smiled.

"I'm so busy now. So many important things to do!" He put down his newspaper and joined Mr. Wong at the table. "Cigarette?"

"No, thank you. I quit."

"Is something wrong with your lungs?"

Mr. Wong didn't reply.

"In case you change your mind, I'll put the pack on the table. Why are you smiling?"

Mr. Wong spat out a tea leaf. "I found a new Friend."

His supervisor lighted another cigarette. "Who is he?"

"Jesus Christ."

The supervisor laughed in disbelief, as if saying, "Did you

find him on the street?"

Mr. Wong's eyes sparkled as he replied to the laugh. "You might say I found Him among the loot on a quiet street in Shanghai."

"Jesus Christ isn't alive!" The supervisor sneered. "Nobody's seen him. He can't be your friend."

"I found two Bibles in a pharmacy when we Chinese were fighting the Japanese." Mr. Wong sipped more tea. "I took them to my wife, who used the high-quality paper making shoe patterns. Then I studied them and found that I have a Friend who cares and who talks to me through His Scriptures."

"Jesus is nothing but superstition. Christianity's failed. It's backward and feudal. The Bible's full of Western lies that the imperialists use as an opiate to benumb the masses. China's responsibility is to rid the country of the barbarian imperialists who pollute our soil. The Japanese foreign devils are gone, thanks to the red-headed foreign devils. Now we must be rid of them too! How can we ever free ourselves from the colonialists if we embrace their religion? Don't you understand, Mr. Wong?" The superior crushed his cigarette in the ashtray.

Mr. Wong poured some tea into his superior's empty cup, then said bluntly, "I wish everyone in China knew Jesus, because He's such a good Friend."

Ignoring the comment, the superior raved on. "China's future is either capitalism or socialism. Who'll win? The Kuomintang or the Red Army—Nationalist President Chiang Kai-shek or the outlaw, Mao Tse-tung, and his peasant army? The Kuomintang's corruption will cause the Nationalist government to fail. Ever since the White Terror massacre, Chiang Kai-shek lost his mandate. It's just a matter of time. Personally, I like Mao's sayings. If we follow the socialist road, we'll reach utopia in China, and, ultimately, the whole world will come to us. Wait and see."

Even though Mr. Wong realized his boss might be a Communist sympathizer or even a double agent, he disagreed. "I believe Christianity can help China."

"We Chinese cannot support the running dogs of the imperialists." The superior's tone was firm. "If you share your superstitious thoughts, you'll become an enemy of the people and subvert their will."

"Maybe the government can help the Chinese people through socialism," Mr. Wong spoke earnestly, "but I think Jesus has the answer for my beloved China." His superior's laugh told Mr. Wong he'd said too much already, so he changed the subject to the purpose of his visit. "I don't think I can work here anymore."

Mr. Wong knew his resignation could be interpreted several ways: Either he thought the Kuomintang would lose, or he feared the Red Army would catch him when it took over the country. He'd be viewed as a rat fleeing from a burning house. Even if his boss didn't understand, he chose to give the real reasons. "I'm not concerned about which government controls China. That's determined by the Real God who lives in heaven. If I keep this job, I'll be expected to take bribes."

Mr. Wong had counted the cost. He knew bribing was deeply ingrained into Chinese culture. The temptation to accept easy money in tough times would be great. Quitting his job meant he'd forgo hospital care, his family would lack security, and his children might starve. Yet his new Friend had promised that his rice and water would be sure.

The superior took a deep drag from his cigarette and laughed defensively, as if saying, "That's the Chinese way! Why fight it? Bribes are like bonuses supplementing the meager wages."

"I'm a Christian now," Mr. Wong explained. "The Bible teaches we should be satisfied with our wages. God wants honest men who stand firm for their beliefs though the heavens fall, so I can't take bribes."

Mr. Wong thought the next laugh from the supervisor declared him crazy! Did he mean, "Don't accuse me of bribery"? Mr. Wong had no desire to point a finger at his boss, so he added, "I'm just telling you why I cannot take bribes."

The atmosphere grew tense as they sat in silence. The superior hastily lighted another cigarette, took long drags, and blew smoke rings. "As to your resignation—" He flicked ash from his cigarette and leaned back in his chair. "You needn't take bribes to work here, but I don't know how you'll ever feed your family without them. If you wish to stay, I'll gladly keep you."

Mr. Wong guessed his supervisor was lying.

"Is your decision final?"

The hopeful tone in the supervisor's voice confirmed Mr. Wong's suspicions.

"It's final." Mr. Wong stood to leave, then decided to share with his boss another reason. "Bribery's only one reason."

"What's another reason?"

"I've decided I can no longer work on the seventh day. I believe it's a holy day to celebrate with my new Friend Jesus and the Real God. I cannot work on the Lord's Day."

The supervisor laughed as he rose to his feet. The laughter implied that Mr. Wong was lazy. "You're just a guard—you don't do anything but sit around and watch for trouble." He stepped around the table.

"I need to have my mind free for spiritual thoughts. As long as I'm guarding, my mind is on evil rather than good."

"Mr. Wong, your resignation is accepted."

"I'll go now." Mr. Wong walked toward the door.

"You'll get no salary!" His boss laughed.

Mr. Wong knew his supervisor was punishing him for his new belief in Western superstition. The laugh meant, "We true Chinese are too practical to worry about trifles like whether or not to accept a bribe; everything revolves around money." His boss had no respect for a Chinese too lazy to work seven days a week to support his family.

As Mr. Wong reached the door, his boss asked, "You'll never find a job in which you can follow your impractical ways. How will you support your family without money?"

This question had troubled Mr. Wong for some time, but he had made his decision. "My Friend Jesus will provide all our needs. He who clothed the lotus blossom will clothe my family," he answered.

As he entered the hall, he heard a fiendish laugh, as if his boss had shouted, "You poor wretched old fool!" Later, his former boss would soften and put in a good word for Mr. Wong, helping him to land a new job as supervisor of the guards inside the Wah tung Garment Factory itself. There he could work, as supervisor, with Sabbaths free.

Chapter 7

A WARNING AND A RAID

After the Japanese surrendered in 1945, Mr. Wong had worked at the WahTung Garment Factory as a supervisor of the guards. Since then, times had changed in many ways, not only for Mr. Wong but for everyone else in China.

He longed for another child to fill the emptiness left by the little daughter he'd sent away with Soong. In due time Lu gave birth to a girl they named Lin. Soon after, Lu began to show signs of tuberculosis. Mr. Wong, who attended church on Sabbath instead of working, earned too little to give her proper medical care. Happily, the church members visited Lu and provided medicine as they could.

On the national level, Nationalist president Chiang Kai-shek had lost to the Red Army and fled to Taiwan. China gained a new constitution. Mao Tse-tung, chairman of the Communist party, controlled China with an iron fist. The government had taken over the WahTung Garment Factory, renaming it the Shanghai Province Garment Industrial Office. Mao planned to squeeze capitalism, imperialism, and Confucianism out of Shanghai and replace them with socialism, communism, and Maoism. Shanghai became a test tube for Mao's ideals. Getting all his cogs to mesh would take time. Until then, neither the city's lifestyle nor Mr. Wong's way of life altered significantly.

To maintain control, the Party had to learn who was loyal. They began on the spiritual plane, expelling missionaries to Hong Kong. Former Chinese Christians publicly confessed to the Communists that they'd been deceived by the missionaries.

Mr. Wong suspected that these "rice Christians," who'd attended church only for the rice bowl served after the sermon, had reported his words and deeds to the government. Feeling that under Communism they no longer needed Christian welfare, they gave up God, salvation from sins, and a chance at pure character development. Surely God had winnowed away the grasses and kept the rice plants, as Jesus had said in Matthew 13:24-30. Mr. Wong felt sad to see the church shrink.

Fearing that organized Christianity might form an opposition, the government encouraged Christians to join the Three-Self Church, which united all the churches under one roof. Three-Self stood for self-governing, self-supporting, and self-propagating. The Communists thought that without foreign aid and management, Chinese Christianity would die. They planned to control the Three-Self Church, infiltrating it with Marxist ideology, making self-governing a fantasy. Because the government church worshiped on Sunday, Seventh-day Adventists went underground, initiating "house churches."

Before liberation, forty women in Mr. Wong's garment factory organized knitting classes. Many nights, Mr. Wong preached to them about his Friend Jesus. About half professed to believe. When the Communists took over the factory, several women reported him to the government, which told him to cease. He didn't listen.

One Friday as he walked down an aisle flanked with workers bent over black sewing machines, Mr. Wong noticed that his assistant, Comrade Zhou, followed him—and guessed what was up.

As supervisor of the guards, Mr. Wong belonged to the garment factory's administrative department, so he'd been able to get Sabbaths off easily. In an effort to change him, the government had lowered his wages to that of a laborer, though they'd allowed him to keep his administrative position. Mr. Wong knew he was little more than a figurehead, but that didn't bother him. He valued the eternal wealth that he could store in heaven.

His assistant, Comrade Zhou Ying, an elderly Communist party member who'd participated in the Long March with Chairman Mao, held the real power in the administration. He monitored Mr. Wong's actions with increasing effectiveness, nagging him about his weekends.

"I don't understand you, Comrade Wong," he said, once he caught up with him. "You take a cut in salary every weekend because you refuse to work Saturdays, but your wife is sick and you have many mouths to feed. Why don't you work Saturdays and provide for your family? Consider what your future will be if you don't reform and join New China."

Many times Mr. Wong had told Zhou Ying that he attended church on Sabbath, explaining that the Real God's followers would be recognized by their Sabbath worship. In the last days, he'd often said, the dragon, who symbolizes the devil, would become angry with the seed of the woman, who represents the church, and would try to devour her offspring, those who followed his Friend Jesus and kept the Ten Regulations. Knowing any conversation with Comrade Zhou would mean repeating his explanation, Mr. Wong headed for his office, replying over his shoulder, "You know my answer."

"You need the time off to attend church."

"Right! I want to spend time with Jesus, my Friend."

They entered the office. Mr. Wong sat at his desk and took out a pair of unfinished cloth shoes he was making as a surprise for Mei-Mei because he couldn't afford to buy shoes. He hoped to make a pair for each member of the family. He'd already mended a slightly damaged pair for his wife that he'd found in the trash. "When you have a friendship with a person," Mr. Wong continued, "you must spend time with him." He picked up a needle, threaded it, and pushed it through the cloth.

"You're a good man and a good worker, Comrade Wong. I'm your friend, so I must warn you."

Mr. Wong didn't look up from his sewing.

"Your superstition is dangerous." Comrade Zhou lighted a cigarette and exhaled a cloud of smoke. "Why do you cling to it? Your wife is ill, yet you refuse to work Saturdays. Think of your family, Comrade Wong, not Jesus."

"Jesus is my Friend. My family comes after Him. He not only changed my life, but He's coming back soon, and I must be ready for Him."

Assistant Zhou's laugh advised Mr. Wong to keep silent. Yet he continued. "Jesus can change your life too. I used to be an impulsive gambler, with two wives. I quarreled with them over money. I don't know how they tolerated me. But that all changed when I met Jesus. Over the years, my Friend has made me a better man."

The assistant laughed again. "Stop talking about your Friend and start working Saturdays. Your family is suffering, and you haven't got enough money to feed or clothe your three children. Your behavior will get you into a lot of trouble one of these days."

"My Friend Jesus will protect me from danger." Mr. Wong sounded brave, but he feared he'd be arrested someday. He decided he couldn't satisfy the government, so he prepared himself mentally for a jail term. His concern wasn't for himself but for his family. He put the cloth shoes away, walked to the door, and added, "The psalmist wrote, 'God's word is a lamp to my feet and a light to my path.' The Real God will honor me for obeying His Fourth Regulation, which is keeping the Sabbath."

"Maybe we can work something out," his assistant said with a smile. "The government will be happy to let you attend church if you report its activities to me. If you agree to my proposition, you can have the time off." Seeing the obvious trap, Mr. Wong refused. To accept might result in the arrests of the very church members who had aided his family. To reject the offer would lead to his own arrest. He left the room to the sound of his assistant's cackle, which meant, "You poor fool!"

Mr. Wong walked down the aisle of sewing machines, inspecting production. "I heard your assistant talking," a worker whispered as he shut off his machine. "What's going to happen to your family if the Communists crack down?"

Mr. Wong smiled. "It's a sign that Jesus is coming. The Old and New Testaments predict that God's people will be persecuted in the last days."

"But how can you survive on a lower salary?" The man adjusted the spool on his sewing machine. "Wouldn't it be better to work Saturdays and get full pay?"

"Ellen White, the prophet of the Seventh-day Adventist Church, wrote that to God, it's better to be dead than to sin.

Thanks for your concern. Since God wants me to spend time with Him on Saturdays, I'll gladly meet the appointment."

"Your church is from America. Do the Americans send you any money?" the worker asked. "What are they doing for you?"

"I'm not a Christian for the rice the Americans might send," Mr. Wong replied. "I've chosen to follow the Real God. My Friend Jesus came to save the world from sin. He'll return, not to destroy the earth, but to restore it."

"I'm afraid the Communists may cause trouble for you if you don't cooperate," the worker cautioned.

Mr. Wong made chopping motions against his throat. "If the government cuts off my head, I won't change," he said. "Remember, we have freedom of religion in our constitution, so they shouldn't cause trouble. Whatever happens, God will provide."

The next Sabbath, Mr. Wong and his family approached Professor Li's four-story house, where a church service was to be held. Lu had not yet accepted Christ, but she had come to realize that some real changes had occurred in her husband's life, and she had started attending Sabbath services with him whenever her health permitted. On this day she was feeling quite well.

Mr. Wong carried a copy of the Old and New Testaments in one hand and the new Chinese constitution in the other, for he never knew when he might need it. Since the Communist takeover, some were confused about the laws, and many were making up regulations as they went along. A copy of the facts was helpful, especially when attending church.

"Is this the house?" Mei-Mei pointed to a house number.

"Let's see." Mr. Wong looked where his daughter pointed. The front of the building, a wall of off-white plaster, had a line of dark brown wooden doors. On top of each door was a small metal plaque with a house number. "Yes, it is!" Reaching behind the plaque, he pressed a doorbell.

Wan Li opened the door, and the Wong family entered. They climbed two flights of stairs and walked through a long hallway. In the living room, Professor Li, an English teacher, sat studying religious books with the aid of a stack of

Chinese-English dictionaries. He arose to meet Mr. Wong. Together they moved the table into the master bedroom.

"Come upstairs and help me set up for our house church," Wan Li urged as he led Mr. Wong and Lee and Mei-Mei up to the fourth story. Picking up the benches stored there, they carried them downstairs into the living room.

They began transforming Professor Li's home into an underground church. The Lis and the Wongs climbed up and down the stairs many times, carrying chairs. They also carried cots to line the walls. They placed rows of benches down the middle of the living room, the master bedroom, and the hallway. Lee set a pulpit beside the piano. The metamorphosis from home to house church completed, Lee and Mei-Mei joined their mother and younger sister Lin. Soon the church members trickled in.

As deacon, Mr. Wong knew that more than church members might come to worship. He welcomed both members and guests while keeping an eye out for troublemakers.

The doorbell rang. Mr. Wong answered it and escorted the new arrivals into the living room, where they found seats. As the congregation assembled, Mr. Wong noticed two younger men who looked suspicious. Were they spies or secret police? He didn't refuse them admittance, hoping they might become interested in God after listening to the service. Professor Li's wife began to play hymns on the piano, and the people sang. More members arrived, until the home grew hot and stuffy. Mr. Wong opened the windows to the balcony.

During the announcements, one of the young men stood and ranted, "The People's benevolent democratic dictatorship will arrest you for your counterrevolutionary activities! Disband your antiparty ways!"

The church service stopped. Apprehension filled the members. Was he a government representative or merely an uneducated rabble-rouser, relishing the power he could wield under the Party's name? Would he take the law into his hands and confiscate everything in the home that wasn't nailed down? Mr. Wong, reaching for his copy of the constitution of the People's Republic of China, pressed his way through the benches to where the young man stood. With a charming smile, he said, "We're doing nothing wrong, my friend. As you can see, we're merely gathering together to worship God."

"You have no right to meet like this against the wishes of the Communists!"

"I'm not aware of that. We live in New China now," Mr. Wong said. "Before liberation, the corrupt Kuomintang army broke laws and cheated the people. We Shanghainese admired the Red Army because it showed respect for people and laws. What we're doing today is perfectly legal."

"There's a law!" the young man barked.

"What law?"

"Marxism, Leninism, and Mao Tse-tung thought declare that religion is the opiate of the people," the young man expounded. "Meeting in this assembly is unlawful. I know the law!"

"You don't know the law," Mr. Wong said bluntly. He pulled out his copy of the constitution and opened it. "Listen to this. Article 35 of the constitution says that the citizens of the People's Republic enjoy freedom of assembly, and article 36 says we enjoy freedom of religion." Pointing to the Chinese characters, he quoted, " 'No state organ, public organization, or individual may compel citizens to believe in or not to believe in any religion; nor may they discriminate against citizens who believe in or do not believe in any religion. The state protects normal religious activities.' "

All eyes focused on the young man. He studied the characters for a long time. Then he looked up, beaming. "We have a law. You shouldn't meet in your home. I'm reading from Article 36: 'No one may make use of religion to engage in activities that disrupt public order!' "

No one moved. They dreaded what the man might do next.

"Let me see that." Mr. Wong reached for the constitution. "Yes, that's what it says, but we're in a private home, so how can we be disrupting public order? I'm reading now from article 39: 'The home of citizens of the People's Republic of China is inviolable.' " Showing the young man where he'd finished reading, Mr. Wong declared, "The government can do nothing against us as long as we practice our own religion in our homes quietly."

Mr. Wong prayed, asking his Friend Jesus to impress the

young man's heart, realizing he might be a judas who'd report him to the authorities.

Abruptly, the young man thrust the constitution at Mr. Wong. "I didn't know," he mumbled. Without another word, he turned to go. Tension left the room with him.

After work on Monday, two policemen awaited Mr. Wong as he was about to leave the factory. "Come with us," one of them ordered. He jerked Mr. Wong's briefcase from his hand and led the way to a black sedan on the street. The other officer opened the back door and pushed Mr. Wong inside so hard that he collapsed on the seat.

"Where are we going?" Mr. Wong asked after they had started down the street.

"We are taking you to the police station," the officer behind the wheel snapped. "We have some questions to ask you."

At the police station, the officers stopped at the front desk long enough to fill out some papers, and then they escorted Mr. Wong to the back part of the building. They stopped at a heavy metal door, opened it, and ordered Mr. Wong inside. The only furnishings were a bed attached to the wall and a toilet.

"Let's see your red card!" one of the officers ordered.

Mr. Wong pulled out of his shirt pocket his work-unit identification folded inside a small red plastic folder. He handed it to the officer, who flipped it open, examined the red seal on the right and the picture on the left, and pocketed it. "You'll get this back if you cooperate."

"Open your briefcase!" another officer ordered. When Mr. Wong obeyed, the police noticed three books written by Ellen G. White. "Give them to us to evaluate."

Mr. Wong obeyed, thinking that the guards who censored his books would read about the Real God. An officer grabbed his briefcase and left. He guessed that he'd have to stay in jail till they found an excuse to prosecute him. An hour later someone shoved a plate of food through a slot in the door. Mr. Wong ate in silence.

When he had finished swallowing the last bite of food, several officers entered his cell. "Comrade Wong, we want you to write out a confession. Give us a detailed autobiography that explains everything you've ever done or said. Tell us about your work, your family, and the people in your church." They handed him paper and notebooks. "If you need more paper, knock on the door, and you'll get some. Now get busy." The police turned to leave, but stopped at the door. With fierce eyes, they threatened, "Confess all, Comrade Wong, because we know everything already! Tell us about the church members and your colleagues. If your information is useful to us, we'll never arrest you again!"

In the tomblike quietness in the room, Mr. Wong began. He said nothing that could compromise any of the church members or incriminate the workers in the factory, even though he knew his decision would certainly mean his future arrest. His writing became more of a testimony, telling how his life had been changed for the better since Jesus had become his Friend and Saviour. Toward evening an officer picked up his confession.

Early the next day, the police again crowded into his cell. The chief glared at him. "You're not telling us everything. We want to know all about your relationships and activities. Confess your crimes now, Comrade Wong, and the Party will be lenient! Write!" The guards handed him more paper, filed out, and again locked the door.

What more could he write in his self-criticism? He glorified his Christian experience, quoting Scripture. When food appeared under his door, he ate, and when he needed more paper, he knocked. On and on he wrote, reminding the police of the Chinese constitution's guarantee of religious freedom. At the end of the day, when another guard picked up his confession, Mr. Wong felt emotionally drained.

On the morning of the third day, the police chief shouted, "Your future is determined by what you write today. Confess your bourgeois, liberalistic thoughts boldly! Free your mind of superstition and feudalistic dogma. Don't fear your kind government. Report what you know!" As he wrote that day, Mr. Wong betrayed no one but explained the beliefs of true Christians in the Seventh-day Adventist Church.

That night the guards reentered his room. "Comrade Wong,

where is your self-criticism?"

Mr. Wong presented them with the writing he had done that day. One of the guards took the papers. Another handed him his three books. "Here are your superstitious books. Keep them to yourself."

The chief of police motioned toward the door. "Follow me," he said to Mr. Wong. They left the cell, with the officers surrounding Mr. Wong. They walked to the front desk of the police station. The chief sat down at the desk, picked up Mr. Wong's briefcase from the floor, and handed it to him.

Mr. Wong opened the case and searched it. He found almost all the belongings they had taken from him when they imprisoned him. Even his money was there! But one thing was missing—his red card.

"You are free to go now," the officer said.

"I cannot go without my red card," Mr. Wong said.

"How did you like the food?" the officer asked, but before Mr. Wong could reply, he said, "Did you think the government would give it to you free? That food costs money. Pay!"

"How much do I owe you?" Mr. Wong asked.

The officer quoted an exorbitant price.

Mr. Wong realized that he would have to pay nearly all the money in his possession. He also knew that he would not be allowed to leave without turning over the money, so he counted it out and handed it to the officer. The chief of police reached into the top drawer of the desk, drew out the red folder, and handed it to Mr. Wong. "Go!" he said with a wave of his hand toward the door.

As he left the prison, Mr. Wong felt glad. It was far better to pay for overpriced meals than to have his family learn about his execution and be given a bill for the bullet!

Neither his neighbors, his colleagues, nor any of the church members asked him about his arrest. Nobody trusted anybody; everyone feared loud knocks on their doors that could come at any time, day or night.

Bounding briskly up the stairs to his home two at a time, Mr. Wong carried a small package under his arm. The house looked bare. He'd sold some furniture to friends in order to have enough money to feed his family. Mei-Mei sat cross-legged on the floor, knitting a sweater.

"How's MaMa doing?" he asked. As if in answer, his wife coughed in bed.

A loud knocking interrupted them. "Open up! Police!"

"Mei-Mei, quick!" Mr. Wong handed her the small package. "Hide this. It's for you."

The pounding on the door grew louder. Mei-Mei took the package to her room. Mr. Wong prayed to his trusted Friend as he stepped toward the door. He still believed that the legal system would honor the constitutional right to religion. When he opened the door, the police rushed in like water overflowing a dam. Scanning the interior, they shouted, "Don't you feel guilty living in such a big house, Old Wong?"

Mr. Wong said nothing.

"Why haven't you given this place to the People's Army?" the chief of police demanded. "It's big enough! Are you a running dog for the Japanese imperialists or a stinking capitalist roader?"

"Neither, sir, I'm just a true Christian dutifully serving New China as a supervisor of the guards in a garment factory."

"Search the house!" the chief commanded, "but destroy nothing. Someday the army will own this mansion." The police searched the kitchen, but there was little to find. In one of the bedrooms they overturned a table, hunted through Mr. Wong's desk drawers, and peered under the bed where Soong had slept. Finding nothing in that room, they searched the other bedroom, then went to the front room. "Off the bed!" two policemen yelled at Lu, who lay on the large wooden Chinese bed in the living room.

"Please, comrade, be kind to my wife. She has tuberculosis."

"Help her up!" the chief ordered. "We must search under that bed!" Mr. Wong and Lee helped Lu off the bed; then Mr. Wong helped the police lift the bed onto its side. "Search! You'll find I have nothing to hide," Mr. Wong assured them.

"Old Wong, you're guilty of harboring bourgeois liberalization literature," a policeman accused. "We need proof for the People's Court." They rummaged through the meager belongings under the bed—mostly shoes, books, and letters. One of them held up Mr. Wong's Old and New Testaments. "Where'd you get these?"

Mr. Wong told the story about the two Bibles in the pharmacy.

"Why didn't you just leave them where you found them?" the policeman asked. "Didn't you know they contain evil Western propaganda?"

"My wife needed the fine paper to make shoe patterns. Later I read them, aided by a long-distance study course, and Jesus became my best Friend."

The police chief scoffed, "This book is full of superstition."

"The Bible tells the truth."

"That's feudalistic nonsense!" The chief raised his voice. "You should be studying Chairman Mao's sayings. Why don't you have his four red volumes prominently displayed?"

Mr. Wong said nothing. A policeman began searching through the family trunk and pulled out a notebook full of newspaper clippings. He handed it to the chief, who glanced at a few pages. "These are forbidden. Why do you keep them?"

"They fulfill the predictions from the Old and New Testaments of signs of the end of the world."

"What signs?"

"Earthquakes, children turning against their parents, parents turning against their children, wars and rumors of wars, plagues, pestilence—"

"Enough! Tell me, how will the world end?"

"My Friend Jesus will return and take all His children home to live with Him forever in heaven."

"You lie!" the police chief shouted. "You don't want Jesus to return—you want Chiang Kai-shek to return! Admit it!"

"I'm looking forward to the second coming of Jesus Christ, because I want to see my Friend."

"Confess! We'll be easy on you if you confess your crimes!"

"I freely confess that I'm a Christian eagerly awaiting Jesus' return."

"You're not a Christian. You work for the Kuomintang in Taiwan Province!" The police chief spat on the floor. "You're a spy!"

"I'm not a spy."

"You lie! We know about you. You've got connections with the Kuomintang, because you work in their police force."

"I resigned my guard duty at the tower when I became a Christian."

"No doubt you did so in order to go underground."

"Not so. I resigned because a Christian cannot accept bribes."

"You're as clever as a snake, but the People's Court will see through your shallow lies." The chief held up the notebook with the newspaper clippings. "This reactionary notebook is evidence. Without the Communist party, there's no New China! You want the end of the world to come—which means the end of New China—therefore, you are antiparty!" He turned to his men. "Arrest him!"

Two policemen grabbed Mr. Wong's hands, forced them behind his back, and began tying them.

"Must you tie me? I'll gladly go with you. My bag is already packed!"

"Where's your bag?" the chief demanded.

Mr. Wong told him.

"Get it!"

A policeman returned with the bag. Opening it, he inspected the contents, taking out each item. When the bag was empty, the chief commanded Mr. Wong to repack it.

As he repacked his bag, Mr. Wong worried about his wife and children. He'd been unable to finish Mei-Mei's gift. He wondered if his son Lee had enough strength to care for his tubercular mother, Lin, and Mei-Mei. Could Lee become the man of the house in his father's absence? When the bag was almost packed, he asked politely, "What's my crime?"

"You're a hoodlum. You're guilty until proven innocent."

"I welcome a trial by the People's Court. China's constitution allows freedom of religion. I'll be released."

"Old Wong, you've been charged with other crimes! You're guilty of treason." The police chief laughed cynically. "The People's Party makes no mistakes. It would rather put away a good man than miss a bad one. Say goodbye to your family, for you'll never see them again!" He opened the living-room door and started down the corridor. "Men, follow me!"

Two policeman took hold of Mr. Wong. One pushed his head down, forcing him to show submission to the will of the People. Another took his bag. They marched him out the door, down the stairs, and into the night.

Silence, emptiness, and apprehension reigned in the house. Mei-Mei and Lin clung to each other for comfort. Lee stared about the room in a state of shock, attempting to deny the night's events. On the floor, amidst an upturned bed, an overturned table, and ransacked drawers, were scattered bars of soap, smashed tubes of toothpaste, and clothes strewn wall to wall. Their mother's cough broke the stillness. Mei-Mei and Lin put the bed back and helped their mother to lie down. Lee ran off to his room, where he played his violin to soothe his nerves.

Suddenly, Mei-Mei remembered her father's gift. The package was torn and stepped on but otherwise unscathed. Picking it up eagerly, she hastily ripped apart the paper covering. "Oh, look!" she squealed as she took out a pair of unfinished shoes. She found a note in one of the shoes. "I wanted to make shoes for all of you before my arrest. . . ."

Mei-Mei fought back tears.

Chapter 8

NEWS OF THE END OF THE WORLD

Mr. Wong's face felt puffy and swollen from a beating the night before. A guard grasped his hair, forcing his head downward, symbolizing his submission to the People's will. Power in the judge's hands, more valuable to the Party than money, would decide whether a prisoner lived or died.

Mr. Wong's legs ached from being forced to stand during days of interrogation. He longed to sit but knew that he must stand throughout the trial. His body felt like one enormous bruise. He'd waited long for trial, enduring anxious prison days. Now the time had come. He was in court at last. That in itself brought some relief, for something could be decided.

"Criminal Wong," the judge said in a monotone, "you are a supervisor at the Shanghai Province Garment Industrial Office. Is that correct?"

"Correct," Mr. Wong replied.

"We have evidence that you are also a Kuomintang spy."

Recent newspapers had featured the execution of nationalist spies. Crowds had watched their fellow Chinese, accused of treason, being shot in the head. Unless proven innocent, Mr. Wong knew the judge's charge could mean his death. A guard yanked on Mr. Wong's hair, pulling his neck back so he could answer the judge. Despite the jerk, he managed to speak firmly, "I'm not a spy."

"I hear you've been talking about Jesus."

Mr. Wong looked into the judge's stern face and said, "Jesus is my best Friend."

Laughing, the judge jostled some papers on his desk. "Here's proof that you're rumormongering about the end of New China." He held up the notebook that the police had confiscated from his house the night of the raid and a copy of *The Spirit of Prophecy* by Ellen G. White. The judge read a quotation Mr. Wong had clipped from Arthur S. Maxwell's book *The Atomic Bomb and the Last Day of the World*. "You want us destroyed by an atomic bomb. Is that what you mean by the end of the world?"

Mr. Wong knew that by "world," the judge meant China's Middle Kingdom, not the entire globe. "I don't think of atomic destruction," Mr. Wong replied. "I don't want anyone killed by the atomic bomb. Jesus wants to rescue everyone. All who follow the Testaments will be saved, for they tell us to be good, not bad."

"You're very cunning. Of course, we all know this Jesus is a code for Chiang Kai-shek, and you're a running dog for the feudalistic Nationalist government." The face of the judge resembled stone, void of expression. He spoke with power. "Are you going to stop talking this treacherous nonsense?"

"I can't stop talking about Jesus, who is my good Friend, if that's what you mean."

"Then you're a traitor!" the judge shouted.

"I'm a Christian."

"So was Chiang Kai-shek," the judge retorted. "He betrayed the People's Party. Admit it—you want Chiang Kai-shek to return, not Jesus. You're a Kuomintang spy—confess!"

"I'll confess my religion." Mr. Wong thought of how Paul, on trial before kings, witnessed for his faith. Perhaps God had brought him to the court so this judge could learn of the spiritual struggle for his mind. "If you read my clippings about the end of the world, you'll see quotations from the Bible and Ellen White's book *The Conflict Between Good and Evil*."

"That's code for the conflict between the Kuomintang and the Red Army," the judge interrupted. "You think that counterrevolutionary, Chiang Kai-shek, is good and that our Great Helmsman, Chairman Mao, is evil. Admit it!"

A guard jerked Mr. Wong's hair on the back of his neck, snapping his head backward, and shouted, "You're a spy who's guilty of rumormongering! Admit it!"

The roots of Mr. Wong's hair stung his neck, but he defended himself. "I'm not rumormongering."

"Where did you get this book? It's published in Hong Kong. You're distributing reactionary propaganda that goes against the will of the People." When the judge said "People," he really meant the Communist government under Chairman Mao.

Mr. Wong replied, "I wrote to the Seventh-day Adventist Church, Hong Kong branch, requesting a copy. They sent one to me."

"The Seventh-day Adventist Church is connected with the American emperor, which means you spy for the enemy! Admit it!"

Mr. Wong reaffirmed, "I have no connection with America, and the message in my notebook is not rumormongering."

"Then what's the message?" the judge asked with feigned politeness.

"*The Conflict Between Good and Evil* tells of the battle between Christ and Satan for the control of this planet, not just China. Seventh-day Adventists believe that its author, Ellen White, was a prophet who wrote messages for our church in the last days. Her book and the Bible predict what will happen before Jesus returns."

"I asked about your reactionary notebook." The judge held it up. "What does Ellen White have to do with this?"

"The newspaper clippings I pasted in the notebook are stories showing how her predictions and those in the Bible are coming true. I'm not a spy but a true Christian who's a Seventh-day Adventist deacon in Shanghai. I believe the teachings of the Old and New Testament and Ellen White. I know the Chinese constitution guarantees freedom of religion. When I compiled my notebook before my arrest, I was exercising my constitutional rights. Seventh-day Adventists in China believe the Bible and the writings of Ellen White. We believe in the soon coming of Jesus, the end of the world, and celebrating the Sabbath. My notebook is legal according to the Chinese constitution, so I appeal to you, do your constitutional duty and release me."

The judge turned the pages of the notebook. "You seem loyal to the government, Comrade Wong," he said. "Your appeal to the constitutional right of religious freedom is justified, comrade. Therefore, the People's Party will drop the charges and release you! But I warn you: proselytizing is illegal and is therefore bourgeois liberalization. Don't talk about Jesus, Ellen White, or the end of the world to anyone. Keep your beliefs to yourself."

Mr. Wong's feet seemed not to touch the street as he walked home a free man. The Real God had overruled! Soon he'd see his wife. He could raise his children as Christians, provide for their needs with his salary at the garment factory, serve as a church deacon, and tell everyone about the end of the world. First, he needed to share the story of God's victory in court with a friend and fellow church member, Professor Li.

Reaching up behind the metal house number at the top of the door, Mr. Wong pressed the doorbell hidden behind the number. Thirteen-year-old Wan Li opened the door and welcomed Mr. Wong. The professor sat in the living room preparing for his next English class.

"I've got a story to tell you!" Mr. Wong announced. He loved storytelling. Vividly, Mr. Wong described every detail: the raid at his home and the discovery of the notebook, the arrest, the trial with his defense, and the release. "God wanted me to witness to the Communists, like Paul." Mr. Wong exclaimed.

"You were accused of spying?" the professor asked.

"That's right." Mr. Wong sat on a chair. "But the Lord was with me. I'm sure the trial was God's plan."

"You're a marked man. Maybe you should be more careful."

Mr. Wong searched his fellow church member's face and asked, "Did Peter quiet down when the priests forbade him to preach Christ's resurrection? My arrest is another proof that we live in the end time." He paused and smiled. "It's my duty to proclaim from the highest mountain that Jesus is coming soon." He tipped his head, brought the side of his hand against his neck, and feigned chopping it off. "I don't care if the government cuts off my head," he said. "I won't stop!"

Chapter 9

FASTING AND A BASKET OF EGGS

The house seemed bare as Mr. Wong looked for something he could pawn. He had sold three watches to the Communists cheaply. That money was gone. A man from the factory had offered him only two renminbi for his purple copper heater. That cash, too, was spent.

His pay had been cut sharply, and he also lost his bonus because he wouldn't work on Saturday at the garment factory. Since he persisted in attending church, the government punished him by lowering his pay to thirty-five renminbi, which was impossible to live on. Two years after his arrest in 1950, a third daughter, Little Doll, was born. He cherished his youngest daughter, who was as beautiful as her name. Unfortunately, she contracted a nerve disorder at age two. She'd spent months in the hospital, until Mr. Wong had insisted, against the doctor's advice, on taking her home. The doctors claimed she would die without proper medical care, but Mr. Wong had faith that God would heal her. At home, she did not die but miraculously began recovering. However, she was another mouth to feed—and he had less money. How could he manage? Then an idea struck him.

Sitting beside his wife's bed, he confessed, "I have no money for food. Maybe I can ask Mr. Shu to loan me some money until I get paid."

Lu objected, "You claim to be a Christian and want a good reputation. If you borrow money and then can't pay it back, you'll give Christianity a bad name. Even if we have no food, we can't borrow money."

Mr. Wong agreed and knelt beside his wife's bed. "Shall we pray about it?"

"If you think it'll do some good." His wife smiled.

He prayed, "My Friend Jesus, You told us in Matthew not to worry about what we eat or drink. You promised that Your Father knows everything I need. Tomorrow is Sabbath. I want it to be special for my children. I'm leaving everything in Your hands." That night, he didn't sleep well, worrying about the health and survival of his children.

The weight of his youngest daughter, Little Doll, bore down on Mr. Wong's shoulders the next day as he walked past the row of sycamores that led from the church to his home. Lee, Mei-Mei, and Lin tagged along behind his wife, Lu. Love made his burden light because he valued the family time on the walk. Little Doll's small legs weren't strong enough to endure long walks at his pace, though he'd slowed it to fit Lu's weakness. Little Doll's previous bout with pleurisy, emphysema, and other complications, collectively diagnosed as a type of tuberculosis, occasionally caused spasms and loss of coordination, so he often carried her. Her weight seemed insignificant compared to the mental and spiritual weight he carried that afternoon.

Little Doll reached out her hand and covered his face. He pulled it away from his eyes, not wanting to run into the pedestrians who crowded the sidewalk. "Daddy," Little Doll said, "I'm hungry. What are we going to eat when we get home?"

Mr. Wong looked at his wife and felt sad. His stomach growled, for the walk added to his healthy appetite. He thought about his prayer the night before and answered, "I'm sorry, Little Doll, but right now we have no food."

"Why, Daddy?"

"Because when Daddy takes the family to church, the factory docks my salary. The government hopes to force me to stop worshiping. That's why sometimes we don't have enough money to buy food."

"Is today one of those sometimes?" Little Doll asked.

"Yes, dear."

"That means we can't eat today, doesn't it?"

The family trudged along in silence for several blocks. Mr. Wong wondered which system his children preferred, Communism or Christianity. He feared that hunger might persuade them that the Communists had a point. Suspecting that Little Doll would whine, he sent up a prayer for an answer.

His daughter broke the silence. "Daddy, I remember we read about fasting in the Bible. Didn't it say that it's good to choose a day not to eat any food and fast?"

"Yes," Mr. Wong replied. "We all sat around MaMa's bed for evening worship while I read what the Bible says about fasting to keep the mind clear when praying."

"We have no food, so why not call this a fast day?"

"Praise the Lord!" Mr. Wong exclaimed. "God must have inspired you to say that! Out of the mouth of babes." Courage replaced his gloom. If he were arrested and separated from his family, that kind of faith would keep his children true.

"Yes, Little Doll, that's a good idea. We'll dedicate today as a fast day. What do the rest of you think?" He looked from his wife to his son, Lee, then to Mei-Mei and Lin. "Does everyone agree with Little Doll?"

Enthusiastically, they decided, "Let's fast!"

Immediately, the whole family seemed to stand a few millimeters taller, and the burden of placing one foot before the other lightened. Lee, Mei-Mei, and Lin ran ahead instead of lagging behind. Even Lu seemed to walk faster.

And fast they did.

In the evening, they heard a knock. Surprised to see Mr. Shu, the man he'd considered borrowing from, Mr. Wong invited him to join the family around Lu's bed. When he was about to leave, he handed an envelope to Mr. Wong. "I felt impressed to give you this." After Mr. Shu left, Mr. Wong found fifty renminbi inside. Showing the money to his wife, Mr. Wong exclaimed, "It's a miracle! God has answered our prayer! Now we can eat—all because we were willing to fast." When times got tough, the family retold the story of when Little Doll turned disaster into joy by suggesting a fast instead of grumbling.

A knock on the door told Lu she had to drag herself out of bed and struggle down the corridor to open the door. Using all her energy, Lu realized tuberculosis had taken its toll. Exhaustion restricted her from cleaning house and cooking food, but she could still dress herself, though it took longer each day. She felt terrible that she couldn't help her husband with the household chores and worried she'd become a burden on him.

When Lu opened the door, she saw an elderly man carrying a basket. "You don't know me," he introduced himself, "but I'm Comrade Zhou, your husband's assistant chief of the guards at the garment factory."

"Come in," Lu said. "Would you like some water?" She led him into the kitchen and began to boil water.

"I'm worried about your family," the colleague said. "I don't know how you can survive on your husband's salary." Lu remembered the walk from church on empty stomachs when Little Doll suggested they declare a day of fast because they had no food.

"I believe your husband brings these hard times upon himself," he said, "because he insists on his radical ideas of attending church every week." The water boiled. With difficulty, Lu poured some into a teacup. Mr. Zhou sipped the steamy liquid. "I think you and your husband need to have a long talk. If he stops clinging to his superstitious nonsense, he'll have the money he needs to provide you with medical care. You're only going to get worse. Who'll take care of you? Think of your future. Your husband can't—or won't! All because of his feudalistic concepts about some Friend he calls Jesus!"

Lu remembered how she had resented Christianity at first. When her husband sent Little Sister Soong away and devoted himself solely to herself and the children, she had accepted his choice for him but not for herself. However, she had seen the changes in her husband and allowed him to study the Bible with her. She had accompanied him to church when she felt able, but she hadn't considered Christianity for herself until after she had developed tubercular symptoms. The church members had come regularly to give her medicine and warm clothes when Mr. Wong had been too poor to buy them. Their kindness and her husband's separation from Soong tipped the scales in favor of her becoming a Christian at some future date. She admired her husband's firmness in his beliefs.

"I'm afraid for your husband." The assistant interrupted Lu's reverie. "By resisting the will of the People, he's traveling down a very dangerous road."

Lu suspected that this was a veiled threat. Her guest reached for the basket and said, "Aiya, I almost forgot to give you this." She looked inside and saw that it was full of chicken and duck eggs. "I want to show you that the government cares," he said, betraying to Lu the fact that he was a Party member. "We know Comrade Wong doesn't earn enough to buy eggs, so we brought these for you."

"Thank you, but you didn't have to," she said politely. Nevertheless, she took the basket when he insisted. She knew he wouldn't give her something unless he wanted to purchase her emotions or curry favor from her. This was only the beginning. He would present scarce commodities in abundance, hoping she would want to return the favor. It was an old Chinese custom.

On his way out the door, he paused. "I believe you have a good chance to influence your husband. With your wifely wiles, you can dissuade him from pursuing his feudalistic path, which will surely lead him to hell." Then he lowered his voice. "I really need your help, because the Communists assigned me to change his mind, but he's so stubborn. They're suspicious I'm too old to be revolutionary, even though I accompanied Chairman Mao on the Long March, so they may terminate my membership in the Party. I want to remain a member, so please talk to your husband. Persuade him to give up his God for me."

After her guest had left, Lu felt disgusted. Comrade Zhou was an old man. Her traditional instincts told her to respect him, but her initial sympathy vanished when she saw his selfishness. The basket of eggs hadn't been a show of government concern for the family. The intent was to turn wives against their husbands, one of the signs her husband had told her that signified the end of time. The basket of eggs was actually a form of persecution. It placed pressure on her to join the Marxists' class warfare against her husband.

She compared his actions to that of the church members. When they became aware of her tuberculosis and their family's inability to afford health care even after government discounts, they gave money. Their gifts, given from the heart, begged nothing in return, even though she wasn't a church member.

Happily, the eggs were hers regardless. She cracked a few over her wok and laboriously stir-fried them into some rice. When her husband arrived, he helped her serve the meal. Lee and the girls joined them.

As he ate, she told him, "Your assistant chief of the guards came by and asked me to urge you to join the government and forget God. He gave us a basket of eggs. That's why you're eating eggs in your rice today." Mr. Wong scowled and rolled his eyes. She knew he didn't like the government encroaching on his religious freedom. "You have no way," she cautioned. "Today's visit is just another warning of trouble, but I'm your wife." She meant she supported him in what he thought right.

Mr. Wong lifted his bowl of fried rice and duck egg to his chin, shoveling the food into his mouth with his chopsticks. From the top of his eye, he saw his children eating in the same manner. The meal was one of the best the family had eaten since payday.

The government was closing in on him. If he didn't change, the party would tighten its pressure. He shuddered, wondering, as his wife's health deteriorated to the point of leaving her bedridden, how he could care for her. He knew that by normal standards he would not have enough money to support his family unless he gave up his God. That he could never do! Somehow, the Real God he trusted would provide a way for his family to survive.

Chapter 10

A ROLL OF RENMINBI AND AN ANGEL

Mr. Wong joined the crowds of people standing in line to buy tickets at the train station. Would the slow-moving line make him late to work and cause more money to be docked from his already meager salary? His financial crisis seemed unbearable. Against his better judgment, he had borrowed money from a sympathetic colleague. Now he had an appointment to meet him to return the cash. Everything depended on buying the ticket in record time, meeting the colleague on time, buying the return ticket quickly, boarding the return train, and arriving at the factory in time to avoid being penalized. His concerns included the uncertain availability of tickets, the slowness of the train, and the long stops en route. If anything failed, his family would have to forego another meal.

Reaching into his pocket, Mr. Wong took out a wad of paper money. Counting it, he separated seven renminbi from the rest, rolled up the paper, and placed it into the pocket of his blue Sun Yat-sen jacket.

Eventually, he reached the counter. A moment later, ticket in hand, he pressed his way into the waiting room. People were sprawled on wooden benches. Some sat atop their meager luggage. When the shrill voice of an attendant announced the train's departure, the people moved toward the gate. Soon another attendant opened the gate, and everyone tried to squeeze through at once. Those in back pushed, making the line flow like a stream toward the gate. Once on the other side, Mr. Wong dashed onto a hard-seat section of the train. Some passengers adjusted their luggage on overhead compartments made of fishnetlike material while others placed their bags on the littered floor. Some passengers had to sit on their bags or on the floor. Mr. Wong leaned against a seat back.

A few jerky minutes into the train ride, Mr. Wong reached into his jacket pocket to make sure his roll of seven renminbi was still there. To his shock, the pocket was empty.

Quickly, he felt his trouser pockets. Empty! He double-checked his jacket pocket to no avail. Had he dropped the money on the train, in the waiting room, at the ticket counter, or while he was in line? Worse yet, had it been stolen in the rush to board? Seven renminbi seemed enormous to Mr. Wong. Besides, if he didn't deliver the money on time, the colleague might accuse him of stealing and never lend him money again. His greatest concern was a late arrival for work, resulting in docked pay!

Mr. Wong squeezed through the crowded car, searching the aisles and under the seats and tables.

"Please, Lord," he prayed silently, "help me find the seven renminbi I promised to return. I celebrate Your Sabbath, even though I need the money for my family. I promised to pay him today. What will he think of Christians if I tell him the money was lost or stolen?"

At the next stop, Mr. Wong got off the train and waited in line to buy a return ticket. Back at his starting point, he searched everywhere for his roll of renminbi. In his intensity, he failed to notice a beautiful young woman staring at him.

When he saw her, she smiled and said, "What are you looking for, Uncle?" In postliberation China, the choice of one's words betrayed attitudes. The Communists insisted that everyone call each other comrade. Calling him Uncle, even though he was a stranger, showed respect for an elder, an honor seldom observed since the Kuomintang's defeat. "Uncle" sounded like music to his ears. Noting her pure, soft skin, Mr. Wong thought she resembled an angel.

"I've lost some money and can't find it anywhere."

Reaching into her purse, she pulled out a roll of brown paper. "Is this it, Uncle?" She offered it to him.

He could scarcely believe his eyes! The money was exactly as he had rolled it! Eagerly he took it from the woman's hand, which he noticed was deformed. He counted the bills. "Seven! It's my money!"

Wondering for a moment if she might be an angel, he asked, "What's your name?"

"Mei-ling," the woman replied.

"Thank you, Mei-ling," Mr. Wong said with a smile. "You must be an angel sent to answer my prayer. I'd love to talk to you sometime." Suddenly he remembered his errand. "But I have to hurry to catch my train. Could you give me your address?"

"Sure, Uncle." Mei-ling hastily scribbled her address and presented it respectfully with both hands to Mr. Wong. The train blew its whistle, and Mr. Wong scrambled toward it.

The following Sabbath after church, Mr. Wong decided to visit Mei-ling. He pressed through crowds that flowed like ants clad in monotonous blue suits and blue caps. Eventually, he came to a house bearing the street name and number that Mei-ling had given him. He knocked on the door.

Mei-ling answered. "Uncle! You came, as you promised."

Mr. Wong entered. "I came to see the angel of the railway who answered my prayer," he said.

Mei-ling laughed courteously. "You can see I'm no angel, Uncle." Immediately, she disappeared and returned with tea. After pouring the tea, she gave him a puzzled look. "Today is Saturday. Don't you work today, Uncle?"

"No." Mr. Wong smiled. "Saturday is the Sabbath of the Lord. I work six days, but on the seventh day I celebrate God's creation and worship my Creator."

"So you're Christian."

"Not only am I Christian, I'm a Seventh-day Adventist Christian."

"That's good," Mei-ling mused. She poured more tea, talked briefly about her family, and asked, "Tell me all about your family, Uncle."

That Mr. Wong loved to do.

When he was through, Mei-ling said, "Oh, Uncle, I'd love to meet your family. Could I have your address?"

He wrote out his address and handed it to her. She thanked

him as she folded the paper. "What does your wife do?"

"My wife has tuberculosis. She can still dress herself and cook a simple meal, but she spends most of her day lying in bed coughing."

"I'm sorry, Uncle." Mei-ling showed sincere concern. "Why doesn't she go to a hospital?"

"She's too weak. She's been unable to walk to the hospital and pick up her medicine for years." He sipped some tea. "I need someone to take her, but my children are too young."

Mei-ling looked down. "Why don't you take her, Uncle?"

"I have to work. Besides, I can't afford it. Since I don't work Sabbath," he explained, "my salary is docked, and I can't get a bonus. That means I lose half my paycheck."

"What are you doing for her?"

His face lighted up as his eyes twinkled. "The kind church members collect offerings from among themselves. They buy whatever they think she needs, mostly medicine, and bring it over. But they can't raise enough to pay the hospital fee."

"Don't forget the government pays half the bill," Mei-ling reminded him.

"I can't pay the price even after the subsidy. Twenty renminbi a day is too much," he stated. "I'm a poor man, Mei-ling, with five mouths to feed and only half an income. Because of my religion, the government views me as an enemy of the People."

"I feel sorry for your wife."

"She's dying, Mei-ling, but maybe God wants to preserve her from the troublous times ahead. The signs of the times indicate that the dragon, that old devil, knows his time is short, which makes him furious at God's people. Jesus is coming soon, and I must spread the good news of salvation from sin." Suddenly, he looked at his watch. "I must see how my wife is doing."

As Mr. Wong headed home, he marveled that this young woman could be so kind—almost like an angel—and yet not be a Christian. Truly Jesus said, "I have sheep that are not of this fold."

The next day, Mr. Wong had a surprise visitor: Mei-ling. "I've come to care for your wife, Uncle," she announced.

"Thank you, Mei-ling." Mr. Wong smiled. "It's very kind of

you to offer, but I can care for her myself."

"She's alone all morning, with no one to care for her when you're at work. Your children don't know what to do. You need my help."

"No! It's impossible, but thank you! I'm happy you're willing, but I mustn't bother you. There's no need for you to come." He meant his refusal, but he didn't wish to explain.

"I must come."

Mr. Wong realized that Mei-ling wasn't just being polite. She really wanted to help him. "Thank you, my daughter, but please don't come."

"You need someone to take care of Auntie."

Mr. Wong decided it was time to explain. "I'll tell you, Mei-ling, honestly. I'm very poor. I don't have enough money to buy eggs or vegetables to eat with our rice. We don't even have oil. How can I pay you?"

"Never mind, Uncle," Mei-ling insisted. "I don't need money, but your wife needs a nurse."

Suddenly, Mr. Wong understood. God had a plan for him to lose his seven renminbi so he could meet a human angel to help him care for his dying wife. "When will you come, Daughter?" he asked.

"Tomorrow."

When Mei-Mei awoke the next day, her father had left for work. She was surprised to find a strange woman sitting by her mother's bed. Her round face resembled her mother's. Mei-Mei watched as the stranger helped her mother dress. She loved the kind voice of the stranger who called her mother Auntie. Then Mei-Mei's eyes riveted upon the crooked fingers on the stranger's left hand.

The stranger smiled down at her. "Which little girl are you? Let me guess. Are you Uncle's eldest daughter?" Blushing, Mei-Mei ran toward her mother. Then Mei-ling said, "How are you, Mei-Mei? My name sounds almost like yours. I'm Mei-ling."

Dumfounded, Mei-Mei wondered how this stranger knew her name. Who was she?

"I'm going to care for Auntie while Uncle's away. Your father told me your name and all about you. He calls me his 'railway angel,' " she laughed, "but I'm very human."

Mei-Mei's mother began a coughing spell. Instantly, Mei-ling handed her a tissue and began wiping her brow with a damp cloth. "Can I help?" Mei-Mei volunteered.

"I'd love your help." Mei-ling beamed. "I need some water. Go get me two basins—one empty and one full of water, please."

Mei-Mei hurried to obey. Mei-ling placed the basins on the floor by Lu's bed. Squatting, she dipped a hand towel into the water, wrung it gently, and placed it on Lu's body. Then she removed the towel and wrung water out of it into the empty basin, repeating the process until Lu was able to breathe more easily.

Leaving Lu to rest, Mei-ling took Mei-Mei to the kitchen and poured boiling water into a teacup. "Take this to your mother," Mei-ling directed, "and give her this medicine."

When Mei-Mei returned to the kitchen, the floor was wet from mopping, and Mei-ling was scrounging through the supplies. "Where do you keep the vegetables?"

"We don't have any," Mei-Mei answered.

"What do you usually eat?"

"Steamed rolls and steamed rice. When we have no rice, we fast."

"How can you eat plain rice?" Mei-ling exclaimed. "There's no flavor."

"It's no problem." Mei-Mei didn't want to say they were poor. Squatting down, Mei-ling said, "But you need meat and vegetables."

"We don't eat meat because we're vegetarian," Mei-Mei replied. "We eat nothing that crawls, hops, swims, flies, or breathes."

"I can get vegetables," Mei-ling said, "but I'll need your help."

Just then, Lin poked her head into the kitchen and stared up at Mei-ling. "That's my sister, Lin," Mei-Mei volunteered.

"How are you, Lin?"

Lin stood frozen, caught between flight and fright, with an extra measure of curiosity thrown in. "I'm going shopping," Mei-ling said. "Would you like to come along?"

Mei-Mei strapped Little Doll to her back. Lee, the oldest, remained behind to care for his mother. Like ducklings following their mother, Mei-Mei and Lin fell into line after Mei-ling.

The streets of the open market were tightly packed with wooden tables and crates loaded with produce. Squatting peasants and standing fishermen shouted loudly in competition with each other. The girls looked longingly at bags of peanuts, watermelon seeds, noodles, and tofu strips.

Mei-ling, looking at the vegetables, explained, "Because we don't have money to buy vegetables, we need to get them without paying."

"How do you do that?" Lin looked up at Mei-ling.

Mei-Mei wondered if Mei-ling expected them to steal.

Mei-ling squatted beside one of the vendors' wooden stands. "Look down here," she said, "and tell me what you see." Lin wrinkled up her nose and said, "Garbage."

"Look again, Lin," Mei-ling said as she picked up some of the yellowish leaves Lin had dubbed garbage. "See, some of these leaves of bok choy and nappa cabbage are only wilted. They'll revive in water!"

Mei-ling paid one mao for a plastic bag and asked, "Who do these leaves belong to?"

"Nobody."

"So, let's take them." Mei-ling stuffed the withered and yellow vegetables into the bag, then gleaned more, careful to choose ones that hadn't actually been on the ground but had lain atop other vegetables. Mei-Mei and her sister stared at her in disbelief. Mei-ling bought two more plastic bags and told the girls to search elsewhere for withered vegetables that were suitable to eat.

The girls ran off and soon returned with their bags full. "When some of the vendors saw what we were doing, they gave us vegetables they couldn't sell," Mei-Mei reported proudly.

At home, Mei-Mei helped Mei-ling cut out yellow parts of the vegetables, soak the fresher parts until they became firm, then place the resurrected food on the counter beside the stove. Selecting a variety of vegetables, they boiled them, placed them in bowls, and served them with steamed rice and steamed rolls.

Mei-Mei and her brother and sisters thought it the tastiest meal they had eaten in weeks.

While they were eating, they heard Mr. Wong coming up the steps talking to someone about the signs of Jesus' soon coming. Mei-ling dashed to the kitchen, with Mei-Mei close behind, and covered the remaining uncooked vegetables with a newspaper. Mei-Mei surmised that Mei-ling wanted to prevent the unexpected guest from seeing the wilted food, which would cause her father to lose face.

Mr. Wong swung the door wide open and allowed his guest to enter first. Seeing Mei-ling in the kitchen, he exclaimed, "God sent my railway angel to care for my ailing wife while I'm at work!" He introduced Mei-ling to the guest, who was a church elder, and told the story of the lost renminbi at the train station. "She has offered to take care of Little Doll when she has her nerve spasms, to take care of the other children, and to cook and wash and clean as well. I like to call her our railway angel in the flesh."

A few days later, as Mr. Wong headed home after a hard day's work in the factory, he noticed a circle of blue-clad men talking together and glancing his way. Straining to listen, he heard one of the men say, "His wife's dying, but he can't be decent enough to bury her before he takes in his new wife!"

The circle dispersed as Mr. Wong approached. He realized the neighborhood believed Mei-ling was his second wife, not a nurse for his wife. He'd never dreamed he'd be so misunderstood, nor had he thought he'd be considered polygamous after he'd sent Soong away and become a deacon in the Seventh-day Adventist church. He'd never thought of Mei-ling as a future wife. Though pure and innocent, he knew that in China a person is guilty until proven innocent.

Surely, he thought, the head of the Neighborhood Committee could help him. He hurried to the man's house.

A stooped old man with wrinkled skin and a toothless smile welcomed him in, then shuffled back to his living room. Inside, Mr. Wong discovered a panel of old maids and elderly widowers.

"You came to talk about Mei-ling," one of them said.

Mr. Wong suddenly realized he'd walked into a planned trap. The rumormongers had conspired with the Neighborhood Committee. He stated simply, "I heard rumors."

"In Old China you could have many wives, but this is New China. Liberate yourself from polygamy, and the rumors will cease."

"Mei-ling is not my second wife. She nurses my wife."

"How convenient!" Mocking laughter burst out.

As Mr. Wong sat down, the Neighborhood Committee arranged the chairs into a circle. In struggle sessions, he knew that an "us versus them" mentality arose; people who agreed with the government criticized the person who was expected to change. If the accused didn't cooperate, the accusers could turn violent. He braced himself by praying to his Friend Jesus.

"We know you're tired of your first wife and have already taken your second," his accusers claimed. "Confess! Admit your guilt! Abandon your counterrevolutionary desires to suppress women and subvert the socialist road."

"Look at my record," Mr. Wong urged. "I'm not counterrevolutionary! I sent away my second wife, Soong, long before liberation. I don't believe in polygamy."

"Then what's a second woman doing in your household?" the Neighborhood Committee demanded. "Doesn't she give you special favors?"

"Such thoughts haven't crossed my mind. I'm a true Christian. I think about things that are pure."

The Neighborhood Committee laughed.

"To me," Mr. Wong continued, "she isn't a wife, but like my daughter."

"You lie! You're a ruffian with two wives," the head of the committee shouted. "Confess the truth!"

An old maid added, "We have a law. Having two wives in New China is forbidden! Stop your bourgeois liberalistic activities!"

"I've told the truth."

At this, the committee became frenzied, demanding he tell them what they wanted to hear. Their words sounded repetitious and their tone unreasonable as they called on him to confess and repent. Mr. Wong stopped listening. He could see no reason to concede to the Neighborhood Committee's demands. All at once, a Bible text came to mind.

"You've taught me something," he announced, leaning forward in his chair. His accusers quieted down to hear his confession. "I now realize my danger in allowing Mei-ling to stay with me. We Christians believe we must avoid the appearance of evil. I haven't avoided that appearance. If anyone thinks I'm a polygamist, I need to change. Mei-ling cannot live with me anymore."

Broad smiles broke out on the faces of the committee members, and the struggle session ended abruptly. Mr. Wong chatted a moment, then left. But on the way home, he dreaded telling Mei-ling the news and worried about who would care for his wife.

"Uncle, I have news from my family," Mei-ling said excitedly as Mr. Wong entered his house. "They've arranged for my marriage and want me to return home for a wedding. I've taught everything I know to Mei-Mei, so she can take care of Auntie and Little Doll." After a pause, she continued, "Uncle, I never thought I'd get married because of my withered hand, but soon I'll have a family of my own."

"I'm very glad for you, Mei-ling. I'll never forget my 'railway angel' sent by God to care for my wife and Little Doll. You also taught Mei-Mei what you know." Mr. Wong marveled at God's timing. "I'll miss you, but the time has come for you to go."

"I'll miss you too, Uncle." Mei-ling sounded sad. "And your family. Maybe I can visit from time to time."

"You'll always be welcome," Mr. Wong assured her. Tearfully, Mei-ling bade farewell to each family member. As she left, a lump in his throat told Mr. Wong that her departure symbolized the end of an era in the Wong family. His Friend Jesus had given Mei-ling to his family when they needed her and taken her away at just the right moment. He marveled at the ways of the Real God. He provided for their family's needs in a way that had far surpassed his wildest imagination. Mei-ling had indeed been a miracle!

Chapter 11

THE WOMAN ON THE BRIDGE

Stepping into the bank with a Bible in one hand and his passbook in the other, Mr. Wong enthusiastically asked people in line, "Do you know my Friend Jesus?" The people glared at him, because he was a stranger defying Chairman Mao's recently issued anti-superstition laws. The Great Helmsman wished to take New China on a Great Leap Forward into "pure communism." To talk any philosophy other than Mao's sayings could result in a prison term or a bullet in the head. Mr. Wong was a protruding nail asking for a pounding because, unlike everyone else, he didn't carry a volume of Mao Tse-tung's Red Books or proclaim their wisdom.

Ignoring their disdain and the probability of arrest, he persisted. Turning to Exodus 20, he explained, "My Friend Jesus has only Ten Regulations." After reading them aloud, he pulled out two copies of the Ten Regulations from the pocket of his Sun Yat-sen suit and offered one to each of the men standing on either side of him in line. When both accepted, he suggested, "Memorize these Ten Rules. They're what Seventh-day Adventist Christians believe."

"Aren't you afraid?" the man behind him asked. "It's illegal to proselytize, yet you talk openly!"

"It's an honor to talk about my Friend Jesus, regardless of whether an earthly ruler passes a decree saying I cannot," Mr. Wong said in a loud voice. Some heads turned. An uncomfortable silence permeated the atmosphere. A teller stared at him, but he continued. "The world's end is near. These laws against religion are a sign that my Friend will return to rescue those who keep the faith and His Regulations. Besides, the Chinese constitution promises religious freedom. Whatever happens to me, God will protect me."

The man in front of Mr. Wong deposited his money and dropped his copy of the Ten Rules into the spittoon. Mr. Wong withdrew an amount from his account and turned to leave. The man behind him had crumpled his copy of the Ten Rules and dropped it onto the floor. Though his message had fallen on stony ground, he was undeterred.

Leaving the bank, he walked through the shopping district on Nanjing Road toward a park, watching for people with whom to share his Friend. He followed Zhongshan Road, paralleling the busy wharfs along the Bund. The bridge that spanned the winding Whampoa River looked dark and foreboding. In the dimness, he noticed a well-dressed woman standing on the bridge looking down at the tugs, junks, and ferries cutting in and around each other.

Sensing danger for a woman to be out at night, Mr. Wong headed toward the bridge, thinking he might help her by sharing the good news about his Friend. His concern heightened when she left the bridge on foot and boarded a ferry. With his anxiety mounting, Mr. Wong bought a ticket for only a few fen.

On board, he searched for the well-to-do woman in the soft-seat section but couldn't find her. He stepped down to the lower deck. She wasn't among the passengers jammed together on rows of wooden benches. When he found her, she was standing in the back, looking very out of place and nervous.

She wore a fur jacket, gold necklaces, jade bracelets, and several gem-studded rings. Her painted face, unlike most in postcapitalist China, looked as if she were going to a banquet. Maybe her husband was a former capitalist who'd failed to escape before the Communists had taken over Shanghai. Approaching her from behind, he surreptitiously held a corner of her coat and asked, "Madame, do you know my Friend Jesus?"

Startled, the woman turned. "What did you say? Who are you?"

"My name's Glorious Country Wong, Madame, and I asked

you if you'd met my Friend Jesus."

She sized him up and down. "How are you, Glorious Country?" Looking around him and over his shoulder, but seeing no one with him, she asked, "Where is He—your Friend?"

"You can't see Him, Madame, but He's here." Mr. Wong smiled. "However, He's coming soon!"

The woman shouted over the wind, "When will He come?"

"We'll never know, Madame, because He didn't tell us the exact day or hour," Mr. Wong explained, "but He gave us signs to look for His coming."

"Who's your Friend?"

"His name is Jesus, and He's the Real God, who developed Ten Regulations to help us live a charmed life here on this earth and later in heaven with Him."

"What are those laws?"

Mr. Wong recited them, and she repeated them after him.

"They're simple to remember," she said as she leaned against the ledge of the ferry, "but there are so many nots, most of which I've done. What happens to people who don't follow your Friend's Ten Regulations?"

"The wages of sin is death, Madame. All have sinned, even me. The good news is that God forgives us and gives us the joy to follow Him now, plus the gift of eternal life." Mr. Wong spoke with enthusiasm. "All of us should die, Madame, but God wants us all to live forever with Him."

Suddenly, the woman placed her head in her hands and spoke with a strained voice. "I don't know why you, a stranger, spoke to me, but I'll be honest with you. Look at that." She pointed over the edge of the boat. The churning water behind the propellers bubbled and splashed against the murky waters on either side of the ferry. "I got on this ferry because I planned to commit suicide. I didn't want anybody to see me, but I guess you'll get to watch me die."

"Ma'am, I wouldn't advise you to take your life," Mr. Wong replied, praying he could dissuade her. He kept his hold on her coat in case he couldn't.

"What does it matter to you?" she retorted. "You don't know me." Pointing to her nose, she declared, "I'm a terrible person.

You don't know all the things I've done. Nobody could ever love someone like me!"

"My Friend Jesus knows all about you and still loves you!"

The woman laughed.

"It's true," Mr. Wong insisted.

"No, I'm going to jump over the side and drown. Then all my troubles will vanish." With a sudden jerk, she tore off one of her gold necklaces, broke it into pieces, and chucked the pieces overboard, wailing, "That's what should happen to me! I can't live under the pressure of the new system. Just leave me alone and let me jump!"

"Madame, what I said is true."

"How do you know?"

"I read it in my Bible." He held up his copy. "My Friend loves you so much He's already died for you so you can live forever with Him. Right now, He's pleading with His Father to blot out your sins if you want Him to."

"What do I have to do?"

"Nothing. Choose to believe. Ask forgiveness for your sins. He'll adopt you as His daughter and help you grow into a new person whom everyone will love. Why, you'll even love yourself."

"How can that be true?"

"It worked for me."

"For you?"

"Yes, Madame, I was once a terrible person!"

"Impossible!"

Mr. Wong told the story of his wealth; of his wives, with whom he quarreled over money because he gambled; and of the Bibles he stole from a pharmacy when he was a sniper fighting against the Japanese occupation. "Studying the Bible changed my life."

"What changes happened to you?"

"I learned from the Bible that polygamy was a sin, so I sent away my Number Two Wife and have stayed true to my Number One Wife. I think soon, as a result, she'll become Christian. She likes how I've changed in other ways too. If I can become a better person because of this Book—" he held up his Bible again— "You can too. Believe me."

The woman, silent for a moment, burst out, "Your talk sounds good, but it's no use. I want to die, for I have nothing to live for."

"If you were to die now, it would be a terrible waste."

"What makes you think so?"

"My Friend Jesus has a special plan for your life if you'll only let Him show you. If you kill yourself, you'll never know His plan."

"Does He care that much for me?"

"He certainly does. He even knew your name before you were conceived, so He knows all about you."

"Really?"

Suddenly, the roar of the engines was cut, and the ferry coasted to the landing. Mr Wong invited her to go somewhere quiet where they could talk more about his Friend.

"Where's your stop?" the woman asked. When he admitted he could get off any time, she looked surprised. "You mean you weren't going anywhere?"

"I saw you on the bridge," Mr. Wong confessed, "and feared you might do yourself harm, so I followed you onto the ferry so I could tell you about my Friend Jesus."

"You did that for me?" The woman was visibly touched. "If what you say about your Friend is true, I'm afraid to take my life without first knowing His plan for me." She asked Mr. Wong for his address in case she wanted to talk later. He scribbled it onto the back of his ticket.

"Goodbye, Glorious Country, I'm going to catch a rickshaw and go home," she said. "I have a new Friend who loves and needs me!"

Mr. Wong returned home, glad he'd helped at least one person. He felt rewarded that his Friend had enabled him to both save her physical life and open the door to save her spiritual life. The evening had been well spent, even if his activities were against the law. He remembered the words of Jesus, "It is lawful to do good."

That night, Mr. Wong was telling his wife and children the story of the woman on the bridge when he heard a knock at the door. When he opened it, the wealthy woman, her hair still mussed from the ferry ride and her makeup smeared, stood before him. She wore a big smile.

"Glorious Country! After we left, I felt terrible because I forgot to thank you." She presented gifts.

"Don't thank me; thank my Friend Jesus." Mr. Wong politely refused the gifts but invited her inside. "Come see my family. They'd love to meet you." He led her down the hall to where his wife lay. "This is the woman I saw on the bridge," Mr. Wong announced, and his children gathered to meet her.

"Glorious Country," the woman began, as she sat on the corner of Lu's bed, "what can I do to thank you for saving my life tonight? How can I repay you?"

"You don't owe me a thing," Mr. Wong replied.

"No," she insisted, "let me give you something. I'm a very rich woman, so I'll give you anything you need."

"The Real God gave you life, not I." Mr. Wong smiled.

"How much does it cost?"

"God's gifts are free."

The woman looked around the room and seemed to notice the missing furniture. "Please, let me pay you. Nothing's free!"

Mr. Wong remembered the story of the leper Namaan, who visited the prophet Elijah and his servant Gehazi. Elijah refused Namaan's gifts, but greedy Gehazi ran after him to receive payment. Mr. Wong knew he could use help from this well-to-do woman. Not wanting to be a Gehazi, however, he replied, "You're right, Madame, God's gifts aren't really free—they'll cost you your miserable, sinful life. He paid for your life of sin by dying on a tree that you might live with Him in eternity. All He asks is that you live your new life for Him."

She smiled. "You're a sincere man, Glorious Country. I see I can give you nothing. Please thank your God for me."

"You can do that for yourself," Mr. Wong suggested. "Why don't we thank Him together now." Everyone stood in a circle while Mr. Wong prayed. Then the woman prayed, thanking her new Friend Jesus for sending Mr. Wong to prevent her from committing suicide and for giving her His free gift of eternal life.

Chapter 12

LU'S NIGHT OF GLORY

The light outside Lu's window dimmed into darkness. Sliding the paper door open, her daughter Mei-Mei entered the room to help her mother undress and prepare for sleep.

Accomplishing anything had become increasingly difficult as tuberculosis weakened Lu. She coughed up increasing amounts of dried blood, and she struggled for each painful breath. Lu knew she couldn't live much longer. Mei-Mei returned with a basin of hot water and began rubbing her mother's body with a cloth, the way she'd learned from Mei-ling. Lu felt sorry that her daughter had never had an opportunity to be a child, but she was proud of her cheerful attitude toward responsibility.

Trouble hadn't made Lu bitter. Thanks to the kindness of the church members and her husband's loving devotion after putting away his Number Two Wife, Lu had altered her opposition toward Christianity. She'd been deeply moved when her husband went beyond duty to care for Soong's livelihood—at great cost to himself and his family.

After her husband's baptism, she gradually began to understand his Bible teachings. Due to her deteriorating condition, she could no longer attend church, but her husband regularly conducted family worship by her bedside, which the children enjoyed. When she couldn't participate, she just lay back and let the message of the hymns seep into her soul, refreshing it anew.

Suddenly, Lu noticed something peculiar. Night had fallen, but she saw light outside. Youth shot through her veins. Testing her new strength, she sat up in bed and dressed for bed without aid. In amazement, Mei-Mei called to the family, "Come look at MaMa! She dressed herself and sat up without help!"

Mr. Wong and Lee dashed in first. Lin and Little Doll joined them. "How are you feeling?" Mr. Wong asked.

Lu spoke without wheezing, "I feel strong now, and I can breathe easily." At first, her husband appeared frightened to see her surge of strength and hear her clear voice. "I fear that a demon has possessed you, granting you superhuman strength to sit."

"Don't be afraid," Lu assured her family. "I have no devil inside me. The Holy Spirit has surrounded this house." Looking out the window beside her bed, she said, "It's night, but there's light all around our house. Angels are with me. Please listen carefully to what I must say."

The family gathered around her bed. "I don't see any light," her husband said as he peered out the window, "but if you do, we must be standing on hallowed ground!" He reached for his hymnal and led out in worship. Her son coughed slightly between stanzas as they sang, "I'm so glad I'm a part of the family of God."

When the song ended, Lu spoke in a clear, forceful manner that was foreign to her. She was not used to giving advice, and she marveled at the words flowing from her mouth. "Come here, my eldest daughter," she said. Mei-Mei sat close beside her on the bed. Lu continued, "After my death, you and your sisters have to suffer a lot. Jesus will take care of you and feed you."

Then she turned to her husband. "Don't scold the Communist party or hate them. You'll endure much suffering also, but God will arrange everything." He grabbed a notebook from the trunk and hastily scribbled every word Lu said. She spoke for nearly two hours about the future and the hard times to come, alluding to an arrest with a subsequent prison sentence, but mostly she gave encouragement and trust in God's power. Mr. Wong wrote fast, page after page, into his notebook.

Lu turned to her son. "Lee, you'll be the head of the household after your father's arrest, but Mei-Mei will be a strength to you." Her husband kept writing. "Lee, though the responsibility may seem too great, you'll succeed, for God won't require more than you can bear. The government will try to force all of you to give up God and work on Sabbath, but you must remain strong, whatever the cost."

When the words ceased to flow, her husband and the children worshiped beside her bed with more songs, Bible study, and prayer. Kneeling around her, each praised God for the encouragement He had given in Lu's words. Then Mr. Wong sat on the corner of the wooden bed and read aloud from the notebook. As Lu heard the glorious words that she'd spoken, she praised God for her energy and the power of the message. After reading it, her husband reverently stored the notebook in the trunk for safekeeping, saying, "I'll read this often later."

Slowly, the light Lu had seen surrounding the house faded from her sight. She knew the angelic host had flown away to fulfill other duties. Feeling more comfortable than she had in a long time, she lay back and fell into a deep sleep.

Three days later, in March 1958, Mr. Wong knelt by her bed and held her hand as her breathing grew heavier and more labored. The vomiting of phlegm clotted with blood ceased, and a peaceful calm covered her face. His children, sensing the nearness of her passing, gathered around her bed and sang hymns with Mr. Wong until Lu's eyes stared vacantly and her body went limp and cold. Lee had lost his MaMa at seventeen; Mei-Mei, at fourteen; Lin, at ten; and dear Little Doll at only six.

After reading 1 Corinthians 15:51-58, Mr. Wong told the children, "We have hope in the resurrection at the sound of the last trumpet when my Friend Jesus returns and takes the faithful home to heaven. I'm confident we'll meet MaMa again, because the Holy Spirit visited her to bring us all comfort."

Yet he felt troubled that his four children would have to survive without their mother. Also, how could he afford a funeral of twenty renminbi, and ten renminbi for the tomb? The price was higher than his salary. Happily, he was visited by a church member, who, learning of his plight, offered twenty reminbi to pay the bill. Mr. Wong gratefully accepted.

When the ceremony ended, the family returned home to a

lonely house. As Mr. Wong looked at the empty bed, he felt relieved that his wife's suffering had ended, for he knew she couldn't have endured the hard times to come.

Despite Lu's warnings and the anti-superstition laws, Mr. Wong refused to work Sabbaths. He continued talking about his Friend Jesus to anyone who would listen, praying that he could assist someone like the wealthy woman he'd met on the ferry. Yet he knew that each contact could become his judas.

One Friday afternoon at work, the telephone operator knocked on his door. "Phone call for Glorious Country Wong."

He followed her down the three flights of steps and through a courtyard. She entered the small room where she sat taking calls and handed him the receiver through a window. Mr. Wong put it to his ear and yelled, "Whey!"

A distinctive bass voice on the other end of the line called back, "Whey, Comrade Wong, there's an emergency at work tomorrow in the Shanghai Province Garment Industrial Office. As supervisor of the guard, you're needed to help assist in the emergency. Can we count on your help?"

With deep apologies, Mr. Wong answered, "Tomorrow's my Sabbath, the day I spend with Jesus. I cannot work tomorrow."

The voice at the other end grew stronger. "I demand that you help out Saturday."

Mr. Wong refused. The voice became insistent. Mr. Wong declared, "I cannot work on the Sabbath day for any reason, because I have an appointment with the Real God."

The voice declared, "The emergency must be solved tomorrow. You're expected to contribute to the Party when the Party asks."

Mr. Wong politely insisted, "I'll cooperate with the Party six days a week, but not on Sabbath, because it's my day of rest."

The tone on the other end grew abusive. "Comrade Wong," it threatened, "you're walking a dangerous path. You must mend your ways. Come in to work tomorrow, or I'm warning you, the path you choose will lead to hell!"

"I won't work tomorrow!" Mr. Wong replied. Reaching through the window, he put the receiver down. He paid the operator and, since it was late in the day, left work. All the way home he thought about the phone call. It must have come from a high-ranking party member. His assistant manager had probably filed a complaint, and now the noose was tightening around his neck. He felt certain that soon he'd be arrested. The better part of wisdom told him he should prepare for that moment. In her last words, Lu had mentioned that he'd suffer. The phone call signaled that his troubles had begun. Anticipating his arrest, Mr. Wong began packing his belongings. He chose only what he could fit into one suitcase.

His most valued treasure, his Testaments, would never be allowed in prison. He devised a means to smuggle one in and keep it from being discovered, even by potential judases. He tore out the pages from one of his spare Bibles (not one of the two he'd found in the pharmacy) and began sewing them, page by page, inside a cotton blanket that he would take with him on the day of his arrest. Every night after work he carefully stitched more pages within the blanket until he had secured every page. Then he sewed a sheet over the blanket, leaving an opening at the bottom. During the process, he slept under the blanket to ensure that no one discovered his secret.

In the mornings, before he went to work, he ruffled the cover to determine whether the pages might crinkle. If he detected the slightest noise, he distributed them more evenly. Finally, satisfied that his Bible was safely hidden, he began a second experiment. Tucking his hand into the bedcover, he practiced removing a page and sewing in another without removing the blanket from the sheet, which would betray him. Convinced of the security of his blanket, he packed it and a health book called *Medical ABC: Guide for Medical Science* into his suitcase. This, he knew, the Communists would allow into prison. In it he could hide one page of the Scriptures at a time without arousing the suspicion of guards or judases. He carried his bag packed for prison to work every morning and home again at night, reasoning that he never knew the exact hour of his arrest. It reminded him of waiting for the return of His Friend, who would come like a thief in the night.

When Mr. Wong arrived at a meeting of the General Bureau of Organization on July 1, 1958, carrying his bag as usual, his assistant manager greeted him. "How are you, Old Wong?"

This greeting startled Mr. Wong. The Communists insisted that everyone refer to each other as Comrade. Why "Old Wong"? This title of endearment wasn't proper for fellow workers to use. Up till now, despite minor instances of persecution, his colleagues had always called him Comrade, which implied good standing. The loss of the title worried him.

In the smoke-filled conference room, he sat down and helped himself to a cup of herbal tea. When everyone had arrived, the committee began discussing "Old Wong," the title of Comrade still conspicuously missing. Mr. Wong squirmed in his chair, pondering his fate.

"Old Wong, this morning the police gave us a message for you," his assistant manager said. "Since it's not clear what they want, I think it best for you to go to the station to settle the matter."

Chapter 13

PRISON VISIT

Getting up from his chair, Mr. Wong picked up his suitcase with his prison belongings and left the General Bureau of Organization. At the exit, policemen from the ShuWei District, each carrying a gun, slapped handcuffs on him. "I arrest you this instant!" shouted an officer.

As the handcuffs locked into place, Mr. Wong felt peace, remembering Lu's words, "Don't scold the Communist party, and don't hate the Communists. You'll endure a great deal of suffering, but God will arrange everything." Trusting that God had a plan, he hugged his suitcase and let the police push him out the door, shove him into the side seat of a three-wheeled motorcycle, and handcuff him to the seat. An officer kicked the engine to life and roared down toward the ShuWei Police Station.

Mr. Wong's thoughts weren't of himself but of his children, who'd lost their mother four months before and now would have no father to raise them as Christians. Tears trailed down his cheeks. Would he ever see them again? How would they survive in a Communist world without his guidance to steer them from atheism?

Asking for courage, he placed the care of his children into the gifted hands of his special Friend Jesus.

At the station, officers pushed him up the cement stairs and threw him into a cell already crowded with prisoners. Mr. Wong settled in with the others, knowing it might be months before justice would consider his case. In the meantime, he had a captive audience to whom he could introduce Jesus as a Friend.

One week later, to his surprise, two officials entered Mr. Wong's cell, handcuffed him, and escorted him into the court-room. The room was bare except for the guards standing on either side of him, holding his head down, and an elderly judge, Mr. Sung.

"Glorious Country Wong, why are you here?" Answering his own question, the judge continued, "Because you believe in su-perstition! We have regulations to investigate and eradicate superstition, because the People want to know only truth."

"I welcome the study of truth." Mr. Wong smiled. "I'm against superstition too. I hope that after you've investigated my be-liefs, you'll know that the Real God's teachings are truth."

"What's the meaning of your superstition?"

"I don't believe in superstition," Mr. Wong replied. "I believe in Jesus Christ, who gives eternal life."

"You're talking bourgeois liberalistic nonsense," the judge retorted. "If believing in Jesus can grant eternal life, then I'll believe in Him too."

Knowing that Chinese covet longevity, Mr. Wong wondered if God had arranged this trial to give him an opportunity to plant seeds of truth that might sprout. "If you believe in Jesus Christ, you, too, can have eternal life."

The judge glared and shouted, "Glorious Country Wong, how dare you say those words? Do you want to bewitch me? I'll cut off your head!"

"It doesn't matter if you cut off my head. What matters is that you believe in Jesus so you can have eternal life." Thinking of his hero Paul before kings, Mr. Wong raised his head toward heaven and declared, "If I don't speak the truth, then I'm mor-tally afraid of death, and I'll cravenly cling to life instead of braving death. Whatever happens here in this trial, Jesus will judge both you and me in the future."

At this, the judge became so angry that he hit the table with his fist and yelled, "I'll cut off your head!"

"I'm prepared to die any time." Mr. Wong hoped his expres-sion of faith would influence the judge for eternity.

The judge's temper erupted. "You stubborn man," he yelled. "Your arrest has taught you no regret, so you're solely responsible for the consequences! Criminal Wong, you should be sentenced to fifteen years in prison, but in view of your pride, I sentence you to twenty years hard labor far west, in Tsinghai Province."

For an instant, Mr. Wong panicked. He gulped at the thought of being sent to Tsinghai, the most dreaded of China's hard labor camps, of being separated so long from his children. When Lu had said the Real God would work everything out for him, he'd believed he'd be released shortly after his arrest. His mind raced through the words of the Chinese constitution in search of a basis for an appeal. "May I ask you, Judge, do you have any bona fide evidence of my crime? If not, why do you sentence me for twenty years? When I talk about Ellen White, who's a prophet of our church, or I tell people about the signs of the soon return of Jesus, my Friend, or I help publish Mrs. White's books, I'm merely exercising my religious belief. Since the government guarantees freedom of religion, what's my crime?"

"The government won't put a good man to injustice or miss a bad man! Don't question the People's decision or ask too much, Criminal Wong! You must build merit in the labor camp to earn the generous mercy of your government. Do as the guards say, work hard, and learn new thoughts. Follow this advice—for it's the only path for Glorious Country Wong—and you'll be released early. Otherwise, you'll choose the path of destruction." The judge laughed. "I predict that a man as stubborn as you, Criminal Wong, won't survive two years at hard labor." He pounded the table. "Court dismissed!"

So Mr. Wong had no recourse. The two officers pushed him from the courtroom into a detention room. Later they shoved him into a rickshaw and transferred him to DeLanChao, a large prison in Hanko District. Mr. Wong's cell, designed for three inmates, already contained five.

While hoping for a retrial, he had little to do but pray, write out a formal appeal, talk about his Friend Jesus to his cellmates who'd listen, and worry about his children.

At home Mei-Mei wondered why her father hadn't returned from work for several days. There must be some explanation.

Her neighbors seemed to avoid her. Why wouldn't they return her greetings? She grew suspicious when she saw neighbors shut their doors whenever she neared. She saw eyes staring at her from every window.

On the way home from school, Mei-Mei noticed a crowd reading a street bulletin board. Posted was a list of counterrevolutionaries who'd been arrested. Reading with mounting tension, Mei-Mei discovered her father's name. So that explained why he hadn't come home! Now she understood why her neighbors treated her and her brother and sisters as outcast children of an anti-revolutionary. Anyone who befriended them could be branded anti-revolutionary. Mei-Mei and her brothers and sisters were alone, isolated in a difficult world. Her MaMa's words came back to her about the children suffering. But the notice mentioned nothing about convictions, so Mei-Mei could hope. Her hopes were dashed by a notice that arrived in the mail stating that Glorious Country Wong had been arrested and sentenced to Tsinghai hard labor camp. Mei-Mei showed it to her brother and sisters at lunch, and they were aghast.

"Where will they take him?" Little Doll asked.

"Far west, beyond Canton and the Sichuan and Yunnan Provinces, eight thousand li, eight thousand clouds, and eight thousand moons away!" Mei-Mei replied.

"Oh, that's far!" Lin gasped. "If China were a rooster, Shanghai lies in the bird's breast and the hard labor camp somewhere in its tail feathers."

"We may never see him again!" Little Doll shed a tear. "Can we visit him in prison?"

Mei-Mei examined the notice. "Yes, it states a date when family members can visit relatives before their transfer to the hard labor prison."

"Let's not miss it!" Little Doll exclaimed.

After the children bowed their heads and said grace, Mei-Mei asked, "Do you think the neighbors are acting strangely?"

"They don't seem to want to talk." Lee lifted a chunk of rice to his mouth with his chopsticks.

"They never greet me," Little Doll complained, "even when I greet them. I don't know why."

"I think they're afraid," Mei-Mei suggested.

"Afraid?"

"Yes, afraid."

"But why?" Little Doll's almond eyes looked up.

"They're afraid because of Father's arrest."

"But Daddy's done nothing wrong!" Lin protested.

"And neither have we," Little Doll joined in on the protest.

"You're right, but Father's been convicted. They're protecting themselves, for they fear the government and don't want to take any chances."

"It's not Christian for them to act this way," Little Doll piped up.

"Our neighbor's aren't Christians, Little Doll, so we must forgive them. They are practical and do what they think necessary to live another day. Down deep, their only desire is to be prosperous and avoid trouble."

"We can't fault them for that." Lin sipped hot water.

"I'm glad you see it that way, Lin. I agree with you."

"But we're still alone." Lee swallowed and went into a spasm of coughing.

Mei-Mei had noticed Lee coughing over the past months and had hoped it was only a bad cold. His cough sounded so much like MaMa's in the early stages. Could he be coming down with the same disease that had killed MaMa? Why him and not her? She'd bathed her mother and had been at greater risk. Could MaMa's words that she'd be a strength mean she'd soon be nursing Lee?

"How can we solve the problem of being alone?" her brother asked. "To our neighbors, we're poison and untouchable. We don't exist—we've lost face!"

"Yes, Lee, we're alone for all those reasons, but we have each other." Even as she said it, Mei-Mei wondered for how long.

"And we have our Friend Jesus," Little Doll volunteered. "Don't forget Him!"

"The Bible says Jesus will be with us always. We must band together and support each other. We must pray for each other and stand united, or we'll all fall. Can we agree to that?" Mei-Mei didn't want anyone in her family to become a spy for the government against anyone else in the family. Each child pledged union to the others. "Now that that's settled," Mei-Mei said with a smile, "the notice gives us a date when we can see Father. Let's begin planning our visit to him."

Later, they wrapped candy, biscuits, and Chinese medicine into a package to present to their father in prison. Taking the gift, the children left the compound, careful to keep together through the crowds. Lee found the bus stop for No. 13 trolley.

When it arrived, they held onto each other as they attempted to board. Boarding a bus in China is only for the aggressive. The timid wait for the next bus. Not wishing to wait, the children pushed each other on.

The people's bodies pressed so tightly that Little Doll complained she couldn't breathe. All four children had both feet firmly planted on the lowest step, just inside the bus.

The ticket taker looked out the bus window to make sure no one was still clamoring aboard, then yelled, "Whey!" A hissing sound signified that the doors would fold shut, and bodies squirmed even closer together to avoid them. Slowly the vehicle advanced, winding its way toward the DeLanChao Prison.

The children had nothing to hold onto for support as they rode standing. The wall-to-wall bodies pressed against them, propping them up when the bus struck a pothole or made a sharp turn.

At each stop, passengers wanting to get off shouted, "*Shah! Shah! Shah cher!*" to make known their intention. With seemingly no room for movement, bodies twisted and squeezed until those who wished to deboard had succeeded. In the shuffling process, the children found themselves on a large aluminum disc in the center of the bus that, consisting of two cars, was linked at the middle, connected by accordion-shaped rubber walls. The disc rotated whenever the bus turned, forcing the children to shuffle their feet. The wall had no window, so Lee had to count the stops.

When the bus at last reached their destination along the Whampoa harbor where ships bound for Hong Kong docked, the children cried, "*Shah cher!*" and the other passengers pressed together to provide the children a few inches to maneuver. They descended the crowded steps and spilled out the bus door onto the pavement.

They arrived well ahead of their appointment. "Look at the line!" Mei-Mei said. "I had no idea so many have been arrested. I wonder if we'll get to see Father."

"All we can do is wait and see," Lee said as they found their places at the end of the line.

"Do you have the notice with you?" Mei-Mei asked Lee. "We can't get into the prison without it." Lee reached into his pocket and quickly located it.

Though they waited a long time, the line moved faster than they had expected. "Lee, I think we won't be allowed much time with Father," Mei-Mei said. "I wish the line moved slower."

"Let's thank God we can see him at all," Lee replied. "Everyone here has relatives they want to see for the last time."

After several hours, the children heard the guards call their names. They entered the prison doors, and Lee presented the notice to the authorities. Soldiers in green Liberation Army uniforms led them to the visiting center. Prisoners stood in a space surrounded by a round wooden desk. The four children waited while other visitors talked with prisoners. Then they saw their father across the desk. His charcoal hair had turned white! He appeared to have aged twenty years.

"You have ten minutes," a soldier stated.

"How are you, Father?" Mei-Mei and Lin chorused while Lee coughed slightly.

"What happened to your hair?" Little Doll blurted out. Lee wondered what the police must have done to their father to have caused the aging.

"Little Doll! I've been so worried about you!" Their father seemed distracted and nervous. "My worrying has aged me. I need more faith!"

Mr. Wong turned to Lee and gave him a piece of paper. "This is an appeal to a higher court. I appealed in prison, but I don't know the result. Take care of Little Doll. She's only six!" Lee promised, then stifled a cough with his hand.

"We brought you this." Mei-Mei placed the package on the desk, but Mr. Wong hardly noticed it.

"Are you still studying the Bible and *The Conflict Between Good and Evil?*" he asked. His question seemed like a plea.

"We study together around the table," Lin replied, "and in the underground church."

"You're all going to church?"

"Every week, Daddy," Little Doll exclaimed.

"You make me so happy to hear that you're being good Christians in my absence." Their father looked lovingly at them. "If you believe strongly in Christ, as I have taught you, they'll never send you to prison."

"We'll do everything you taught us," Lee asserted, and the girls chimed in their approval, but Lee noticed that Mei-Mei looked over at the guard apprehensively. She suspected their words might be used against them or their father in the future.

"I've been telling people in prison about Jesus coming back, but judases report me, and the guards move me around." Their father spoke quietly so the guards couldn't hear. "Hasn't stopped me, though." He grinned. "The jailer misunderstood and scolded me for telling one prisoner that the atomic bomb is a sign of the end time. He thought I said the American emperor wanted to drop the atomic bomb on China in the Korean War."

Lee covered his mouth to smother a cough.

"Are you all right, Lee?" His father looked concerned.

Mei-Mei mumbled, "He's been coughing."

"Deep coughs?" Mr. Wong coaxed.

"I've been afraid that since I took care of MaMa, I'd catch TB, but Lee's coughing is a surprise." Mei-Mei spoke timidly. "Why him? Why not me?"

"The Lord has a plan." Mr. Wong's strong voice gave courage to the children. "Maybe He wants to preserve Lee from persecution. Lee, take care of yourself. Go to the hospital and get medicine, even if you have to ask for aid from church members."

"I got your gift." Mei-Mei changed the subject.

"The shoes?" her father replied eagerly. "Do they fit?"

"Sure. They fit!"

"I wish I could have given you all new shoes, but—"

"Time to go!" a soldier interrupted.

Mr. Wong spread his arms, and Little Doll ran with open arms to receive her father's embrace, but the soldier stood between them.

"Neibu!" "Forbidden!" The soldier's smile suggested he enjoyed the power of the word and playing authority's game of "let's make a regulation."

"She's my daughter. I may never see her again." Mr. Wong turned to the soldier and pleaded, "May I hug Little Doll one last time?"

"It's forbidden!" The soldier spread the two apart.

Panic spread across their father's face as his arms flayed. He spun around as if to try again to hug Little Doll, yet he knew his time was up. The children watched their father leave the circular desk in such disarray that he forgot to take their package with him.

"Don't forget the package!" Lee called.

A troubled and confused father returned to the meeting area and snatched up the gift. "Take that appeal to the proper authorities, Lee." His words sounded garbled. "The constitution promises freedom of religion, so I've done nothing wrong!" The children, deeply troubled to see their father so disturbed, knew they might never see him again. All hope now hinged on God's will and a retrial.

Chapter 14

PUBLIC TRIAL

A soldier in an olive green Liberation Army uniform marched on either side of handcuffed Mr. Wong as they led him by his hair toward a wooden platform hastily erected outside the DeLanChao Prison. A large crowd of students, gathered to learn politics, stood below the platform, jeering.

Harassing the prisoner, the soldiers shouted, "Shame! Shame!" They punctuated their points with the butt of their metal batons. "You sin against the government yet rebelliously feign innocence by holding up your head!" Enjoying his sense of power, one soldier yanked Mr. Wong's hair, forcing his head downward. Louder they yelled, "You're about to face trial! Soon you'll reap the results of your counterrevolutionary activities."

Mr. Wong felt glad to be marching. He loved long walks, something he'd missed in the prison. He needed the exercise to keep his body and mind strong for the coming trial.

On the platform sat a panel of prosecutors flanking the judge. Mr. Wong knew his fate, for the present, was predetermined by the Chinese government, though ultimately preordained by the Real God. Was this trial the result of his appeal? Would he be released, as he had been once before?

The soldiers pushed Mr. Wong up the steps onto the platform, forcing him to stand facing a sea of stern faces, with his back to his accusers.

"Criminal Wong," the panel began, "why are you here?"

"Because I talk about my Friend Jesus and spend time with Him in church every Saturday."

"Correct."

"The Shanghai Province Garment Industrial Office filed complaints against you." Mr. Wong heard the prosecutor rustle some papers. "They claim you won't work Saturdays."

The judge interrupted the prosecutor. "I don't understand the problem. We Chinese are traditionally hard working, laboring long hours seven days a week! Why won't you work Saturdays?"

"I'll be glad to explain." Unable to raise his head because one of the soldiers held it down, Mr. Wong addressed his toes. "I cannot work on Sabbath."

"What is Sabbath?"

"A day of rest." Thrilled at the opportunity to witness in chains like his heroes Peter and Paul, Mr. Wong silently thanked Jesus for a chance to explain part of the Bible to this judge, the panel of prosecutors, the soldiers, and the crowd standing at the base of the platform. "I'm a true Christian. We Christians are simple people who believe the Old and New Testaments are the Word of the Real God, who gave us Ten Regulations in Exodus 20, one of which says that people can work six days, but the seventh day is the Sabbath. I can't work on the Lord's day. I worship at church."

"Your superstition tells you to do this?"

"Celebrating the Sabbath," Mr. Wong explained in a clear voice, "is one of the Real God's Regulations, which I must obey."

"The Shanghai Province Garment Industrial Office needs you to work," the prosecutor barked. "Don't you think the needs of the office and China are important?"

"I'm loyal to my company and my country, but I cannot work on Sabbath."

"Why not?"

"God's laws precede human laws. To disobey human laws is a crime, but going against God's laws is sin."

"There's no difference between sin and crime!" a prosecutor shouted.

The students yelled, "Confess your crimes!"

The judge continued. "Do you attend church all day Saturday?"

"No."

"Then why must you have the whole day off?"

"The Testaments are quite specific about the Sabbath. Moses wrote in Leviticus that we're to celebrate the Sabbath from sundown to sundown, so the Sabbath is a twenty-four-hour rest period from labor to spend special time with my Friend Jesus."

"So you rest all day?"

"And spend time with Jesus and my family."

"I understand the problem now." Papers rustled again behind Mr. Wong. "You say your refusal to work Saturday is part of your religious belief. I suspect your behavior is harmless and not a crime but more a matter of laziness!"

Someone in the crowd raised his fist and shouted, "You're a no-good worker!" and others joined in.

"But," the judge continued, "in the people's working paradise, many workers want a day off and get it, as long as their request is reasonable. The people know that if they don't want to work, they don't have to. Fortunately, most workers are so grateful to their government, they work extra hard. Before socialism, people were exploited by capitalists and imperialists and resented their work. Today, they sing happily while they work. That's proof that our Great Helmsman, Mao Tse-tung, is the correct leader of the People! But you're an exception. This Sabbath has nothing to do with your superstitious belief. In my judgment, your unwillingness to work is a sign of character weakness. You're a no-good worker. In the people's working paradise, I can't convict you on this point."

Mr. Wong saw a gleam of hope. Maybe he'd be released. He remembered his wife's words that God would work everything out.

"We have other evidence against you. Your government kindly invited your counterrevolutionary children to visit you," a prosecutor began, "but when they arrived, you told them that if they believed in Christ, they wouldn't be put in prison. Is that true?"

"Correct."

"How dare you make such a statement?" the prosecutor demanded. "The government wants to stamp out superstition, yet you try to perpetuate it by deceiving your anti-revolutionary family!"

The mob raised fists and chanted, "Down with anti-revolutionary families! Long live Chairman Mao!"

"My family is Christian, not anti-revolutionary," Mr. Wong countered when the jeers quieted enough for him to be heard. "Christians aren't against the government. We support the government."

"Christianity goes against Chairman Mao's anti-superstition campaign!" a prosecutor criticized. "Join the Great Leap Forward!"

As if on cue, the crowd shouted, "Down with superstition! Down with Christianity!"

Mr. Wong realized the government had two choices: mold him into Maoism or make him into an example for the masses. But to him, this struggle session was an opportunity to share truth. "I'm aware that the government is against superstition, but belief in Christ is not superstition. I don't wish my family to be superstitious. I want them to fully understand and follow the truth. If my family clings to the truths written in the Word of the Real God, they won't be superstitious. If they aren't superstitious, there will be no reason for them to be imprisoned."

"You're as clever as a snake! Who's teaching whom?" a prosecutor shouted. "We're your teachers, Criminal Wong, not your pupils. Just answer our questions!"

"I hear you've been talking about Jesus," the judge charged.

"I have."

"Even after your arrest, you spread rumors from a Christian book by Arthur Maxwell, *The Atomic Bomb and the End of the World*, saying that the atomic bomb is a sign that Jesus is coming soon and that the end of the world is near. The jailer asked you to quit, but you disobeyed. Why do you persist in rumormongering and proselytizing?"

Mr. Wong looked down at the faces in the mob, students about the age of Lee or Mei-Mei, who'd come to learn politics. All the faces seemed made of stone. Did they reflect the face of the judge? While he hoped for leniency, Mr. Wong feared the verdict was predetermined and this was a mock trial. He knew martyrs' blood was seed, so he decided to speak the truth for the sake of the stone faces beneath him, hoping some of the hardness masked fertile soil. "Jesus is my best Friend," he said boldly. "He can be your Friend too."

"Stop rumormongering and talking bourgeois liberalistic nonsense!"

"I can't stop talking about Jesus, if that's what you mean."

"You're proselytizing!"

"I must," Mr. Wong insisted. "We Chinese need to know the truth about my Friend Jesus' hasty return."

"Shut up!"

Mr. Wong stopped talking. He knew the Real God could release him if He wished, but if not, He had a reason.

"Why are you here?" the judge asked again.

"I hope to be released," Mr. Wong replied. "The constitution of New China guarantees freedom of religion. I've done nothing wrong!"

The judge laughed. "The People's government makes no mistakes! How dare you say New China made a mistake?"

"I trust you'll find me innocent and release me."

"You've been arrested, so you must be guilty." The panel laughed in agreement. "Are you innocent?"

"Yes."

"What are you accused of?"

"Talking about my Friend Jesus."

"That's proselytizing! We have a regulation against that," a prosecutor shouted. "The law allows you to believe whatever you want as long as you keep it to yourself, but you can't propagate superstition!"

The mob shouted, "Down with superstition!"

"Jesus told us to talk about Him to everyone. It's part of our religion."

"Will you stop talking about Jesus?"

"I cannot!"

"We have a law!"

"Yo guidin!"

"I know your law."

"Will you obey it?"

"I cannot obey human laws if they violate the laws of the Real God."

104 THE MAN WHO COULDN'T BE KILLED

The masses joined the prosecutor, screaming, "Long live Chairman Mao!" until some grew hoarse. The prosecutor chanted, "Down with the Kuomintang!" The crowd parroted him. The prosecutor yelled, "Down with superstition and counter-revolutionary families!" The mob echoed. The prosecutor sang, "Without the Communist party, China doesn't exist!" and "The East is Red!" Again the masses chorused his words like a deafening choir.

The judge turned to Mr. Wong and said, "Would that you lived up to your name and helped make New China a glorious country. Instead, you've disgraced China!" Then he yelled out to the multitude, "Down with Criminal Wong!" The crowd went wild, repeating the condemnation again and again.

When the commotion subsided, the prosecutors joined the judge standing next to the soldiers and Mr. Wong. From a piece of paper, the judge read, "Here's the verdict from the Shanghai District People's Procurate."

The crowd grew quiet. "The accused, Criminal Wong, male, fifty-one years old, a guard in the former WahTung Garment Factory, is accused of anti-revolutionary activity. After extensive investigation, his crimes are written below: After liberation, his mind remained reactionary. He pretended to be a missionary, but in actuality he was doing illegal activities. The accused is a rumormonger. In 1950, Criminal Wong spread rumors of bad omens and searched in newspapers for stories of earthquakes, floods, and droughts all over the world. He spread the following three rumors: 'Jesus is coming again!' 'The world is coming to an end!' and 'Marxism is inferior to the Bible!' "

"After his arrest," the judge continued, "the accused persuaded criminals in jail to believe in Jesus. He told his anti-revolutionary family the superstitious idea that if they believed in Christ, they wouldn't be thrown in prison. He supported his friend, Mr. Cho, in his efforts to illegally print a book by an American author, Ellen G. White, entitled *The War Between Good and Evil*. Criminal Wong has connections with the American emperor's Seventh-day Adventist Church in Hong Kong, exchanges reactionary books with a Hong Kong publishing company, and propagates these anti-revolutionary books illegally, which proves that he's an American spy! He persists in calling Chiang Kai-shek by the code name Jesus—proof that he's also a Kuomintang spy!"

Now Mr. Wong knew his sentence had been written long before the trial. Charges that had been dropped in his first trial were brought up again. He felt pity for the students who flung mud balls at him. Knowing they'd been deceived by the government's propaganda, he forgave them. He prayed that some might think about his words and want to know more about his Friend Jesus.

"According to his crimes listed above," the judge continued, "the accused, Criminal Wong, is found guilty. He refused to recant after liberation. In an earlier hearing he was sentenced to twenty years of hard labor. I will be kind and reduce that to fifteen years and deprivation of political rights for five years after the prison term." Mr. Wong knew that meant he would spend 20 years in prison just like his previous sentence. There had been no change.

The prosecutors shouted, "Down with Criminal Wong!" and the soldiers and crowd again chanted, "Down with Criminal Wong!"

The judge continued, "Criminal Wong will receive a copy of the verdict before he's transferred to hard labor camp. Criminal Wong, the benevolent dictatorship of the People cannot release you. At the labor camp, you'll be taught the error of your stubborn ways. Maybe under the strain of hard labor, you'll be able to shake off the laziness you call Sabbath!"

The prosecutors spread large sheets of red paper on the platform, took out large brushes and black paint, knelt over the paper, and began painting Chinese characters on each banner describing Mr. Wong's crimes. As they painted a placard, they chanted, "Criminal Wong: Anti-revolutionary American and Kuomintang spy, rumormonger of Western superstition." They tied a string to the placard and draped it around Mr. Wong's neck.

A prosecutor painted the entire verdict in bold characters on a long sheet of white paper. He rolled it up, took it to the bulletin board on the sidewalk beside the police station, and pinned it up beside other banners decrying convicted prisoners. The masses crowded near the board.

With the trial at an end, the soldiers escorted Mr. Wong past the bulletin board so he could see the crowds reading his crimes. Those who couldn't make out the characters gawked at the banner or stared at other people who could read. The soldiers pushed him up the stairs into the DeLanChao Prison and locked him into his cell to await the long journey to the dreaded hard labor camp in western China.

Chapter 15

THE JOURNEY TO THE WEST

A line of flatbed trucks with wooden sidewalls rolled up in front of the DeLanChao Prison. The drivers revved the engines impatiently while soldiers lined up about 1,500 convicts, including Mr. Wong. Each inmate wore a cardboard placard stating his crime tied to his neck. Mr. Wong noticed that most were rapists, robbers, and petty thieves. All had waited months, locked in cells, awaiting trial, which sentenced them to travel overland to serve prison terms in the hard labor camp.

"Come forward!" A soldier chained the arms and legs of ten prisoners to each other. Then he yelled, "Hurry up! March into the truck!" Soldiers beat the convicts, including Mr. Wong, with metal clubs to hurry them as they climbed aboard the back of the truck. Several soldiers joined the offenders to guarantee that none escaped. Prison guards on the ground locked the prisoners in the trucks, gave a signal, and the drivers left.

Many trucks full of convicts and soldiers paraded through the streets of Shanghai. Prison guards in the passenger seats shouted into microphones connected to loudspeakers attached to the roofs. Repeatedly they blasted the neighborhoods, reading the criminals' names, their crimes, and their sentences as the trucks drove by residential neighborhoods, city centers, and former business districts.

Crowds gathered on both sides of the street, clamoring to see the convoy of criminals and hear the words blaring from the loudspeakers. Some in the mob cursed the criminals as they watched the soldiers pound their heads and backs with metal clubs. Others shuddered and struggled to read the blood-red characters written on the placards draped from the convicts' necks.

The criminals drooped their heads lower each time they heard their names called, but not Mr. Wong! Though he hoped his children wouldn't see him and be hurt, he stood with his head held high. He felt no remorse, for he knew he was not a spy. After the trucks wound around the same streets several times, they turned toward the train station. The long road west to the hard labor camp instilled fear in every prisoner. Mr. Wong had never heard of anyone sent to work in a labor camp who'd returned home. Would he, like the others, die in the penal colony? He prayed that he might see his family again.

The trucks stopped at the JiaoWan train station. The guards pushed open the doors of several freight cars. The stench left from cattle, horses, sheep, and goats filled the air. The soldiers gave each prisoner a bag with six pounds of biscuits. "Don't eat them all at once," they cautioned. "These biscuits should last you for the entire trip! You get no more."

The soldiers shoved the prisoners aboard the train. They placed a barrel in the middle of the car. "That's your toilet!" They laughed and locked the doors behind them. The floor was covered with bits of straw and dried dung, coated with fungus. Mr. Wong tried to sit on his bag, but the humiliation of riding as mere animals deeply disturbed him. The train clacked down the track day after day. It would chug through nine provinces to reach its destination. Mr. Wong worried about Lee and his girls, fearful that Lee might join him at the hard labor camp on the next train load.

"My Friend Jesus," he prayed, "You know my tubercular son hasn't the strength to endure hard labor. Don't let him be sent where I am going. May he rest until the resurrection day. For me, either deliver me like Daniel, or let me die like Stephen."

The train made only major stops. Mr. Wong and the other prisoners were unchained and allowed to use the facilities at the major stations. Otherwise, they tried to use the barrel. Some succeeded; others failed. After a few days, the freight car became a human sty, which made Mr. Wong feel utterly disgraced.

As the food rations ran low, prisoners fought with each other for biscuits. Mr. Wong gladly shared his. With little to eat, the prisoners rarely attempted to use the barrel. On the seventh day of the ride, the train lurched to a stop. Guards opened the door and shouted, "Line up! Out of the train!"

Each prisoner vied to be the first one out of the stinking sty that had confined them for a week. Pushing, shoving, and squeezing, they hoped for a chance to escape. But the chains held the criminals fast to each other.

"Get in line!" The guards yelled and beat on the prisoners. "Come out single file!" The mass of wriggling, squirming bodies untangled themselves, formed a line, and filed out of the train onto the platform.

The soldiers marched groups of chained prisoners into the back of army trucks, forcing them to stand, braced shoulder to shoulder, atop their luggage. Mr. Wong and the others supported themselves on each other's bodies. "Don't talk, or you'll be punished!" a guard commanded. "If you need to defecate and can't hold it, yell at one of the guards. We'll stop, but be quick, or you'll be beaten! If you try to escape, a bullet will stop you! Your name will be stricken from the list. Because you rebelled against the benevolent will of the People, we'll bury you immediately, and your family won't be notified of your death. Understand? Cooperate, or you alone bear responsibility for the consequences!"

The trucks roared down paved roads, then bumpy dirt roads, jostling the convicts against each other. Tempers rose and fists came to blows.

The journey expanded into months, with little or no sleep. The rough going wreaked havoc on the prisoners' bowels and bladders. "Whey! Whey!" a prisoner complained, waiting for the driver to recognize him and stop for a bowel movement. The soldiers insisted on being certain the prisoner's request was not to urinate. When the stool stop was granted, others jumped down to take advantage of the situation. The guards kept an eagle eye and severely beat any with the slightest constipation.

During one stool stop, a movement caught Mr. Wong's eye. A prisoner who had just emerged from the latrine attempted a mad dash for freedom. Instantly, a soldier took aim, fired, and stopped him with a bullet. He fell in midstride, transformed into a lifeless clump.

The guards selected strong inmates. "You! And you! And you! Off the truck!" they demanded, handing them picks and shovels. "Dig!" When a trench was completed, the guards ordered the gravediggers to toss the body into the hole and cover it. As promised, a guard struck the prisoner's name from his list. "It's as if he never existed," he declared. "Remember that next time you consider escaping!" Despite the warning, Mr. Wong witnessed others repeat the scenario, with similar results.

Delays for urination weren't tolerated. Most prisoners leaked down their pants, on each other, and dribbled onto their luggage below. Mr. Wong held his cup to catch urine whenever the truck's jiggling aroused the urge. When the cup was full, he passed it to a criminal near the door, who tossed out the contents.

As the truck bounced along, a prisoner lost his footing, creating a domino effect. Criminals stumbled over each other. The cup tipped, splashing the warm fluid on all the prisoners within reach. Some pushed against their neighbors in a vain attempt not to get splashed. Urine seeped through their clothes and clung to their skin, adding its odor to human sweat. The effort to dodge the urine knocked over more prisoners. Many mumbled curses. Convicts stomped on each other's toes and grabbed at each other to gain support. One regained his footing. He became a strong tower for Mr. Wong and the others to lean on until they, too, could stand again. Someone managed to pick up Mr. Wong's cup and return it.

The trip lasted several weeks. Many prisoners died. Whenever an inmate collapsed, the driver stopped, and the strongest criminals threw the body onto the roadside. "We'll notify local authorities, who in turn will notify the families of the death," a guard announced. Without further ado, the journey continued until the next criminal died or a prisoner requested another stool stop.

The truck's bouncing increased. The relentless journey became torture to Mr. Wong—cramped muscles, aching bones, rattled nerves, and standing that caused the blood to flow to his feet. Overcrowded quarters gave him almost no space. If only he could walk—anything for relief from the rocky ride!

Without warning, Mr. Wong's wish was granted. The truck drivers had been dodging rocks that could have gutted the underside of their trucks. Suddenly, the truck Mr. Wong rode in stopped. The driver revved the engines, but the tires only spun, digging in deeper and spraying arches of dirt that spat behind the truck. The guards jumped out of their passenger seats, ran around to the chained prisoners in back, pulled on the nearest bodies, and ordered, "Get out!"

The convicts almost fell out the back. Hardly able to walk, Mr. Wong and the other prisoners stepped on solid ground. The guards unloaded the criminals with their urine-soaked luggage.

Mr. Wong surveyed the vast open spaces, barren and desolate, surrounding him. Distant mountains made him wonder if his new home was outside China. Truly, from overcrowded Shanghai to this remote tundra they had exited civilization and entered a void. To their destination, no roads led. They were blazing a new trail leading beyond nowhere into desolation. Or so it seemed to Mr. Wong.

"The trucks can't go any farther," the guards said as they released the prisoners from their chains. "March, hoodlums! Get into step with the Great Leap Forward. We're marching to Mao's Marxist millennium. This march will help you understand the suffering of our Great Helmsman, Mao Tse-tung, when he battled the traitorous Kuomintang. If you'd been on the Long March with Chairman Mao, you wouldn't be here today." Some guards laughed. "March, counterrevolutionaries! March to your new home!

"Don't think of escaping!" the guards shouted at the mass of bewildered prisoners. "It's impossible! We can easily find you. Some of the grass is poison. If the grass doesn't kill you, diarrhea will. You're safer with us. Without us, you'll surely die! March on, you radicals!"

As they tramped over the flat, barren terrain of Tsinghai Province with clumps of sage-colored grass, the land seemed better suited for nomads, goats, sheep, and yaks. A terrible wind chilled the prisoners. Shivers shot up and down Mr. Wong's spine as he breathed the bitterly cold air surrounding him.

Mr. Wong gasped for breath. Usually a grand walker, he found himself slowing down. His legs wouldn't move fast. The high altitude with its rarified air gave many marchers altitude sickness. Drowsiness struck Mr. Wong, yet he trudged onward. Lack of exercise for so many months had reduced his fitness. The thin air sapped his strength. He longed to rest.

"Don't stop!" a guard shouted to a straggler with a bloated belly. "Hurry up! We've got to get to the camp before nightfall."

"I can't go on!"

"Are you plotting escape?" the guard asked fiercely.

"No. I'm sick. Let me die!"

"Liar!" the guard yelled. "You can't live without us to give you food and drink. You'll die in the wilderness before anyone can rescue you. Get going!"

The exhausted man struggled to put one foot in front of the other. Satisfied, the guard moved ahead. Mr. Wong went over to the struggling prisoner, placed an arm around him, and helped him along.

As dusk approached, Mr. Wong wondered how much farther they had to hike before they arrived at the camp. "Keep marching! The camp is just ahead!" the guards barked. "Join the Great Helmsman's Great Leap Forward. March to Mao's Marxist millennium! Keep moving!"

Mr. Wong could see nothing like a camp looming ahead—not even a form of a building. If the guards said the camp was not far, they knew something they weren't telling him. Yet on they trudged. When it became too dark to see, the guards shouted, "This is the camp. Lie down! Go to sleep!"

No walls. No buildings. Nothing but barren, flat lands and beastly winds. Mr. Wong and some of the stronger prisoners dug in the earth with their bare hands until the holes were big enough to provide warmth and protection from the wind and cold. The weaker criminals dug no holes but slept on the surface, using their body heat to keep themselves alive. Mr. Wong knelt and prayed to his Friend Jesus. Then, lying in his hole against the bodies of other inmates, he shivered through the night until he fell into a fitful sleep, uncertain about the morning.

Chapter 16

A TASTE OF HARD LABOR CAMP

No one was given food the next morning. The guards arranged the prisoners for exercises and roll call and issued communal work assignments.

"Criminals are required to meet daily quotas," a guard lectured. "If any criminal doesn't meet his quota, he'll be punished. There'll be no leniency and no exceptions!" Calling the prisoners by name, he assigned some to dig an underground burrow for living quarters and others to clean out a corral for some neighboring nomads. "Criminals in this unit will pick up the dried sheep, goat, and yak droppings and cart the dung to the camp to be used for fuel to bake bricks and cook meals."

Then Mr. Wong heard his name called. "This unit will make bricks! Each inmate should form five hundred bricks a day or be solely responsible for the consequences."

A guard supervised Mr. Wong's work unit. "First, we need an adobe wall to surround the area," he ordered. They used the dirt from the excavating to form bricks. Mr. Wong felt as though he were an Israelite slave in Pharoah's Egypt mixing straw and mud.

Though they toiled the entire day, no one was given any food. The hungry prisoners salivated, watching the guards eat. Though his stomach ached, Mr. Wong remembered the walk home from church when his family had no food and Little Doll had declared it a time to fast. He found comfort, despite stomach cramps, following his daughter's example and declaring his first day in camp a day of fasting.

At the end of the day, the guards calculated the number of bricks each prisoner had made. Two of the inmates in Mr. Wong's unit had fallen short of their quota.

"What did the superintendent say this morning?" one of the guards barked.

"Criminals should make five hundred bricks," the prisoners replied.

"Why did you disobey orders?"

The guilty inmates said nothing.

"Come with me," the guard commanded.

Mr. Wong watched. The guard led the two prisoners to the hole that had been dug by the cave-digging team. He slapped one of the prisoners on the back of the head. "Take off your shoe," he ordered.

The prisoner took off a shoe and handed it to the guard.

"I don't want it," the guard snapped. "Give it to your friend."

The prisoner handed his shoe to the other inmate, who took it.

"Now bend down!" the guard ordered the prisoner with the bare foot. The inmate leaned over.

The guard turned to the prisoner holding the shoe. "Smack him with the shoe and shout, 'Why didn't you meet your quota?' Don't stop till you're tired. When you need a rest, remove your shoe and trade places with him. He'll hit you and shout about your laziness. Trade off until I give you permission to stop."

The prisoners beat each other all evening until they were exhausted and hoarse. About midnight, the guard returned. "Are you going to meet your quota tomorrow?"

"Oh yes!" they chorused.

"Promise?"

"We promise!" they croaked. "Thank you for teaching us this valuable lesson about quotas! Please forgive us and let us sleep tonight."

"All right, you can sleep now." Relieved, the men put their shoes back on and dragged themselves to a spot out of the wind where they could sleep.

That night, hungry and tired, Mr. Wong talked with his Friend Jesus. "Thank You for giving me the strength to meet my quota.

Help me never to fall short so they can't force me to beat a fellow inmate. May I prove my loyalty to China by being a good worker."

On the second day, the guards served a small ration of highland barley for supper. Though he preferred rice, Mr. Wong was grateful that at least the meal was vegetarian. That night, many stomachs growled from inadequate food and a desire for rice. To the Chinese prisoners, barley was fodder for animals. Rice was never on their menu. Day after day, varieties of barley abounded.

As the excavation on the burrow continued, Mr. Wong's work unit kept making bricks, which they baked in small earthen kilns. In a few days the prisoners began laying the brick into walls. First, they built a high wall around the entire compound. Then, they built a guard tower in the center of the compound that was high enough for the guards to see over the walls. They also constructed a guardhouse and toilet for the guards. The prisoners coated the finished walls with more mud, which, when sunbaked, was brown, with specks of straw poking through.

When the burrow was completed, the prisoners descended a sloping tunnel into their new underground residence, which to Mr. Wong seemed like stepping into the shadow of a grave. Inside, the guards lighted candles. After their eyes adjusted, the prisoners scanned their dimly lighted surroundings. In the center of the massive hole was an open space large enough for all to stand for rallies and announcements. Across from their entrance into the burrow was an exit of equal size. These two openings allowed in a small amount of light. Large, dark niches had been carved into the walls on either side.

"Each of you gets a candle," a guard explained. "We'll assign you by name to the niches in the burrow, with up to fifteen prisoners to a niche."

They called the prisoner next to Mr. Wong first. He came forward to receive his candle. "Give me your bag!" the guard ordered. Searching through it, he removed a blanket. Running his hand over it, he yelled, "What's this?" Tearing into the blanket, he extracted a knife. Holding it into the air, he barked, "You think you can outsmart us? You're wrong! No weapons allowed. Nothing sharp or made of metal—not even spoons. Your belongings will be inspected again every six months."

When Mr. Wong's name was called, the guard took his bag and pulled out the belongings. He felt his blanket and pillowcase. Mr. Wong feared the guard might discover the hidden Scriptures. The guard found nothing. After stuffing his things back in the bag, Mr. Wong proceeded to his niche.

"Niche thirteen is forbidden!" a guard yelled. "The roof caved in. "Some of you will die before your sentence is complete. We'll store your bodies there."

Mr. Wong hurried to his niche. Candlelight revealed dirt walls with no support. Water dripped from the roof. He wondered if his niche might also collapse some night during his sleep. Other prisoners had already staked out their space. Finding an unoccupied corner, he set his bag down. With his hands, he carved a perch in the wall and set his candle on it. The other inmates followed his example. With all the candles in place, he could see to sort his belongings. Some still felt damp with urine from the long trip west.

Mr. Wong set out his precious blanket with the pages of the Testaments hidden inside. Pretending to adjust his blanket, he pulled out a page and stuck it into his medical book. With the aid of this book, he could memorize Scripture when the guards thought he was studying medicine. He vowed never to share his secret with anyone. He needed his Testaments. Without them, he knew he could not survive.

For breakfast each morning, the guards lined up the prisoners in front of their niches. They squatted as the guards served them steamed rolls and cooked greens harvested from nearby fields. Mr. Wong thought mealtime was an opportune time for witnessing. He hoped his fellow inmates would ask him about his Friend Jesus. Like his hero Daniel, who prayed openly three times daily, Mr. Wong determined to do the same. When the guards handed him his steamed roll, Mr. Wong set his plate on the ground, bowed his head, closed his eyes, and thanked God for his meager meal. When he opened his eyes, he discovered his steamed roll and vegetables had vanished.

"Looking for something?" the inmate next to him said.

"My food's gone."

"Did you eat it?"

"No."

"What's the problem here?" A guard came up to Mr. Wong.

"My steamed roll and vegetables are gone."

"What happened?"

"I closed my eyes to thank the Real God for the food," Mr. Wong explained. "When I opened them, my food had disappeared."

"Come with me, Criminal Wong." Mr. Wong followed the guard up the dirt steps that led outside the cave. He saw his vegetables crushed into the ground. The roll had dirty footprints stamped on it. He couldn't eat the vegetables, but the roll was salvageable.

"Pick it up!"

Mr. Wong obeyed. He followed the guard back down into the burrow. "Do you know why this happened, Criminal Wong? Your superstition angered a prisoner. He despised you because you thanked a god who does not exist for the food the government issued you." Everyone heard the guard's loud accusations.

"Your God didn't give you the food—your government did! I'm very disappointed in your ungratefulness, Criminal Wong. Your kind government takes care of the Christians and Muslims in the camp. The Muslims get their special food with enough oil and clean vegetables. They show appreciation for our great favor of kindness by kneeling at our feet and kissing our hands. Why don't you thank your government instead of your so-called Real God? When a prisoner saw your ingratitude toward the Party, he thought you didn't deserve to eat, so he dashed outside and stomped on your steamed roll. Learn your lesson, and give up your superstition!"

"My Friend Jesus made it possible for the government to serve us this food," Mr. Wong answered. "Everything belongs to Him, even the cattle on a thousand hills!"

"The cooks gave you this food," the guard snapped.

Hoping he might get another ration, Mr. Wong looked forlornly at his crushed steamed roll coated with dirt. "Eat it!" the guard ordered. "We have no more steamed rolls today. Eat, or starve!" A few of the inmates laughed. Mr. Wong stuck the filthy steamed roll, in his mouth and started chewing. The bland dough stuck on the roof of his mouth, and grit and dirt crunched in his teeth, but he swallowed it all.

At his next meal, Mr. Wong boldly bowed his head again, closed his eyes, and thanked the Real God for his food. Again his steamed roll was missing.

"Are you persisting in your superstition?" a guard growled. "You're in prison for reeducation, to learn from your gracious government, but you stubbornly refuse to be taught. Go get your roll."

Mr. Wong retrieved his roll, stepped back down into the cave, and ate without complaining.

"How do you like dirty food?" a guard joked. "You know you can end your problem easily. Give up your feudalistic superstition, and you won't offend the prisoners." The guard was right, Mr. Wong thought. He could compromise and say grace without bowing his head or closing his eyes, but then he wouldn't be witnessing.

Munching on the soiled steamed roll, Mr. Wong knew the prisoners had gained merit for stealing his rolls. He could imagine the scenario. When he closed his eyes, a prisoner looked toward the guard. If the guard looked away, he had permission. Quickly he'd snatch the food and dash outside with it.

As the days turned into months, Mr. Wong grew accustomed to the guard's lecture and the jaunt to the surface every mealtime after blessing his food. Though he didn't appreciate gritty food, he knew many watched him. Mr. Wong praised the Real God that more guards and inmates had become aware of his friendship with Jesus.

After six months of eating smashed food, one day Mr. Wong opened his eyes after saying grace and discovered his steamed roll on his plate untouched. He closed his eyes again and thanked his Friend for delivering him from persecution. He could bless his food in peace. Subsequent meals were also left alone. Maybe both guards and inmates had decided there was nothing they could do. How long must he wait before someone would ask him about his Friend Jesus?

As time went on, the menu changed. In addition to the steamed roll, the guards included pieces of coagulated lard and pork in barley meal. Pork could be another way to witness that might encourage his inmates to ask him about the Real God. Greedily, the inmates stuffed the pork and barley with coagulated lard into their mouths, shouting, "This is the first sign of real food we've eaten in months." Mr. Wong ate his steamed roll, but he ignored the pork.

A burly inmate stood up, walked over, slapped him across the face, and demanded, "Why aren't you eating, Old Wong? You haven't touched your barley!"

"I'm a Christian," Mr. Wong explained, knowing others listened. "There's pork and lard in it. True Christians don't eat pork."

"Guard," he shouted over his shoulder, "this ungrateful pig isn't eating."

"What's the trouble?" the guard bellowed.

"This man says a true Christian won't eat pork!"

"Why do you stubbornly cling to your superstition?" The guard bent close to Mr. Wong's face. "Isn't it enough that you thank your so-called Real God for your food? Now you arrogantly refuse to eat it!"

"Shall I help him eat?" Mr. Wong saw the inmate look into the guard's eyes, hoping to gain favor. "We Chinese eat pork and lard. How can you eat without pork? The taste isn't so good!"

"I cannot eat pork or lard," Mr. Wong said. "The Real God taught us that the flesh of the pig is unclean for eating."

"Listen to your fellow prisoners. They give good advice. Eat the pork!" the guard urged.

"It's just little pieces of pork! It won't hurt you." The prisoner picked up some with Mr. Wong's chopstick and put it to Mr. Wong's mouth. "Eat it!"

"I'm sorry," Mr. Wong replied, "but I can't eat even a little bit of lard or pork."

"If you do what your God says and follow the decadent Western influences from the missionaries who brainwashed you, you'll starve to death!" the guard coaxed. "Your God isn't your savior. He's killing you. Give up this deadly superstition—eat pork and live a long time!"

Mr. Wong saw renewed eye contact between the guard and the burly prisoner, which showed that the irritated inmate was itching to rough up Mr. Wong. But to do so, he needed an approving signal from the guard. "Shall I feed it to him? I'll make him eat it."

The guard looked down at Mr. Wong and wrinkled his lips and nose into a sneer. That was the signal the brute needed. "Criminal Wong, learn from your new friend. He seems concerned about you." The guard stepped away a safe distance, but close enough to supervise the prisoners' deeds without taking part.

Mr. Wong sized up his opponent and knew that with his police training and sniper experience, he could win a fight, but that wasn't the Christian way. "My God," he prayed, "stifle my natural instincts. Strengthen me to be a true Christian example."

"I've never met a Chinese who didn't eat pork or lard. You're very strange," the furious prisoner sneered. "Cooperate with me. Just eat it—it's good for you." The prisoner put pork and lard to Mr. Wong's mouth, but Mr. Wong refused to open it. He scanned the cave for the guard who had given the go-ahead look. The other prisoner picked Mr. Wong up and threw him to the ground, then sat on his stomach and reached for the pork. A crowd gathered.

"Don't make it hard for yourself." The prisoner leaned forward until Mr. Wong could feel his hot breath against his face. "Open your mouth."

Mr. Wong refused.

The guard pressed his way through the crowd. "Criminal Wong, you're upsetting everyone and drawing undue attention to yourself. Eat the pork."

Mr. Wong made no move to resist, nor did he open his mouth. He just closed his eyes and prayed silently to his Friend. Then a gruff hand grabbed his cheeks and pressed them together until his mouth opened. The prisoner on top of him stuffed the pork into his mouth. "Eat it!"

Mr. Wong spat out the mouthful. It fell back on his face and chest. "You stubborn old fool!" The inmate slapped Mr. Wong.

"Must I teach you to eat?" He pried open Mr. Wong's mouth and crammed pork into it. Then he pushed his jaw up and down. Sticking his finger down Mr. Wong's throat, he forced him to gag enough to swallow. This he repeated, bite after bite, until all the pork and lard were gone. "How did it taste? Good?" With his task completed, the prisoner looked into the approving eyes of the guard. He stood and stepped away from Mr. Wong, leaving him lying on the ground. "Next time, Old Wong, eat your food yourself."

The crowd dispersed. Mr. Wong had a bad taste in his mouth and pity in his heart. He pulled himself off the ground, walked over to the wall where the men urinated, stuck his finger down his throat, and vomited everything up. His empty stomach and the taste of vomit in his mouth were only slightly better than the pork or lard, but the meat was out of his system. He'd won the fight without swinging a blow.

As the days passed, the quantity of food decreased. At mealtime, when the prisoners assembled in the center of the cave, a guard announced, "Due to circumstances beyond the control of the People's benevolent dictatorship, this region of the country is experiencing a slight draught. Your kind government is unable to produce the rations it desires, so everyone must suffer. We jailers have graciously devised a plan to fill the slack for you criminals. Inmate-physician Lai has searched the nearby fields and gathered edible herbs, berries, and mushrooms. A work unit will be assigned to harvest them, but first Criminal Lai will explain the task."

Dr. Lai explained, "I've identified twenty-seven varieties of edible plants. However, many grasses, herbs, berries, and mushrooms are poisonous." Setting a bag on the ground, he produced a number of plants, showing which ones were edible and which were not. Lifting up a mushroom that looked particularly delicious to Mr. Wong, the doctor declared, "Don't eat this one. It holds swift death! Once ingested, your face will swell, then your neck. By the time the swelling reaches your chest, you'll be dead."

After all the prisoners had examined the plants, Dr. Lai cautioned, "If you want to live long, you must be careful to pick only the twenty-seven varieties I've shown you. Harvesting the wrong plants will lead to someone's death. You could be the unlucky one."

Mr. Wong was assigned to the group that harvested the grass and small plants growing near the prison grounds. A guard gave them machetes and ordered them to cut the grass. They kept their backs bent the entire day as they whacked at the plants. Each prisoner watched the others and tried to harvest a little faster, not from duty, but for fear of being punished if he didn't. Though his stomach felt empty, Mr. Wong maintained the lead.

As the sun set, the prisoners knew they'd soon be escorted back to the cave. When it seemed too dark to cut more plants, they attempted to sort the toxic plants from the edible ones, then cart their harvest to the cave. The correct diagnosis of toxic greens, berries, and mushrooms was imperative, for the food they had gathered would become their evening meal.

Mr. Wong separated a few plants and kept them for himself. Stashing them away quickly, he didn't have time to sort out the toxic leaves and fungi. Returning to the cave, he went into his niche, lighted his candle, sat cross-legged in his corner, and got out his bowl. He sorted through the plants he had kept back and put the nonpoisonous ones in the bowl. Then he poured water in the bowl and crushed and stirred the plants until they formed a mushy cold soup. Just as Mr. Wong was about to eat, a guard stepped in. "Don't eat that!" he scolded. "It might kill you! Don't you know the grass is poisonous?"

"This is the only food I can eat," Mr. Wong replied as he took a sip of his soup.

"What's wrong with the food your government graciously gives you?" the guard snapped. "Today the government was proud to issue its prisoners the best food."

"You know I'm vegetarian, yet you insist that I eat pork and lard. The Christian Bible teaches that not eating meat is better for people. When the Real God created Adam and Eve, He told them they could eat the fruit, grains, and nuts, not animals." Mr. Wong smiled and sipped his soup noisily.

"I know many Christians who eat large pieces of pork! Why don't you Seventh-day Adventists eat meat? We serve you meat because we want to help you give up your superstition."

Though the other inmates appeared to be ignoring the conversation, Mr. Wong knew they were listening. "I cannot give up my Friend Jesus." Mr. Wong sipped some more of his cold soup. "He's the only way to salvation."

"It looks to me as if your superstitious ideas will kill you. By following these feudalistic teachings, you eat poison rather than pork or lard. Your superstitions make you crazy!"

"My Friend Jesus will protect me if I follow His teachings." Mr. Wong swallowed a mouthful of soup. "The Bible tells us that when Paul was bitten by a poisonous snake, he didn't die. I'm not Paul. I may die, but if I do, I know my Friend will resurrect me when He blows His trumpet heralding His return."

The guard laughed in contempt. "How can an intelligent man like you, Criminal Wong, believe those fables?"

"The Bible stories are true," Mr. Wong retorted.

"You're in a reeducation camp to help you distinguish truth from fiction," the guard shouted. "When will you be brave enough to abandon your superstition and embrace New China?" The guard spat on the ground. "If you die from eating toxic food, it's your own fault!"

"The government is kind to warn me of danger." Confident that he had sorted the plants carefully, Mr. Wong smiled; then he tipped his bowl up and gulped down the last of his soup. "Thank you for your concern. I'm sorry I cannot eat the government's pork or lard, but I'll gladly eat the government's vegetables."

Squatting down, the guard sat cross-legged beside Mr. Wong. "Your government wants you to live, Criminal Wong. By serving you pork and lard, it's being very good to you. Poor Chinese can eat cornmeal. They'd give anything for pork to spice their rice."

"I appreciate the government's good intentions and concern for my health, but I choose to follow Daniel's example. When the Babylonian king Nebuchadnezzar wanted Daniel to eat meat and wine, he asked to be fed only rice, vegetables, and water for ten days. When Nebuchadnezzar compared him with the other men in the Babylonian court, he judged him ten times healthier and ten times wiser. I'll be healthier, too, if I'm allowed to eat simple food like vegetables."

"You have the gall to ask special favors." The guard arose and spat again. "Listen to me, Criminal Wong. You'll eat pork and lard tomorrow!" He turned and stormed out of the niche.

The next day one of the prisoners force-fed Mr. Wong, but again he vomited. After working another day in the field, he fixed another bowl of cold soup from the local plants and ate it.

Then the menu changed. Though the other prisoners were given only the local plants, the guards still served Mr. Wong pork with lard, which he refused to eat. However, the prisoners gave up force-feeding him. Mr. Wong maintained a diet of steamed rolls and cold soup.

Some of the other prisoners began to lose weight or bloat up from malnutrition. Their bellies doubled in size, and their faces grew puffy. Some died from eating the vegetables because the harvesters carelessly brought in toxic plants. Their bodies were discarded in niche thirteen. Though his face puffed slightly, Mr. Wong looked healthier than the other prisoners. He even ate the delicious-looking mushrooms that Dr. Lai had warned about but showed no fatal symptoms.

As the days turned into months, Mr. Wong knew the guards were watching, hoping he'd get sick or die from the toxic grasses, berries, and mushrooms. But in contrast to the other inmates in his work unit, who ate the government's rations and became weaker and worked less, Mr. Wong accomplished more in a day's shift, in spite of his insufficient diet. He felt the Real God blessed him for his stand against pork and lard. After six months of harassment, the head of the guards visited Mr. Wong in his niche.

"Have you eaten yet?" The guard's question was a rhetorical greeting. As Mr. Wong mixed his cold soup, the guard asked, "How does it taste?"

"Good." Mr. Wong smiled, sensing that the visit was friendly. "Would you like some?"

The guard refused, so Mr. Wong ate alone. They talked of Christian beliefs and compared the similar views of the two philosophies, Marxism and Christianity. When the topic of work ethic arose, Mr. Wong told the story about the talents. "Each worker was praised or condemned by the king, based on the number of talents he developed," Mr. Wong concluded.

"Marx also taught that each worker should work as he was able," the guard said. "I've noticed you're a good worker."

"The Bible says he who does not work shall not eat."

"I think Marx would have agreed," the guard said. "Is that why you work so hard?"

"Yes."

Looking him in the eye, the guard smiled. "I like you, Criminal Wong. You're a good man. You work hard and deserve to eat well. You're too valuable a worker to lose. Starting tomorrow, I'm going to tell the cooks to fix your meals the way you like."

And he did.

Chapter 17

PRAYING UNDER THE GUN

The wind whipped through the rolling pasture that surrounded the prison walls, chilling Mr. Wong to the bone. With their backs bent close to the ground, the two prisoners on either side of Mr. Wong raced each other to see who could whack the most weeds with their sickles. Working like beasts of burden rather than farmers, they frantically stuffed the "vegetables" into their baskets. Usually the fastest in his group, Mr. Wong hurried. Yet his pace slackened as he avoided the toxic berries, mushrooms, and grasses. He felt concerned as he saw the others toss everything into the baskets, which would be served in their meals.

Without warning, he felt a smack on the back of his head. The pain shot through him. Turning, he saw a guard glaring at him. He slapped Mr. Wong twice across the face, making blood gush out of his nose. "You're a no-good worker!" the guard yelled, forgetting that Mr. Wong regularly finished ahead of the other prisoners.

Anger overwhelmed Mr. Wong. His instincts from his days as a policeman returned. He had once beaten many a man. Fearing he would retaliate, he fell to his knees and prayed, "Dear God, am I qualified to suffer for my Friend Jesus? You know this beating is unfair. Control my emotions. I cannot! Thank God for this blessing. Enable me to be happy to suffer for You."

As he got up from his knees, he felt peace in his heart. Saying nothing, he forced himself to keep up with the others. He remembered the judge's order at his trial in Shanghai about obeying the guards, thinking new thoughts, and working hard to earn a lighter sentence. Since he couldn't obey when the guards ordered him to disobey God, the only way he could prove his loyalty to his government was by working hard. As he toiled at a back-breaking speed, he rejoiced that his children couldn't see him suffer!

Soon the guard announced a lunch break. "Thirty minutes." The weary crew, too distant from the prison compound, sat in groups and ate sack lunches provided for them.

Mr. Wong devoured his highland barley, steamed buns, and vegetables quickly. When he finished, he got out his medical book, turned to the cover page, and meditated on a verse he found on one of the pages he'd torn out of his Testaments. Engrossed, he was surprised to see an inmate sitting next to him.

"Old Wong," the prisoner said, "what can you tell me about your Real God?"

Mr. Wong couldn't believe his ears. Was this man sincere, or was he a judas wanting to earn merit with the guards? He decided to risk sharing Friend Jesus and His Ten Regulations with the man. Since they were beyond earshot of the guards, he wrote out the First Regulation on toilet paper, folded it, and handed it to the inmate. "Read this," he said. "It's one of my Friend Jesus' Ten Regulations. When you've memorized all the words, destroy the paper. Repeat the verse by memory to me, and I'll give you the next one." Mr. Wong believed that if the prisoner memorized the verse, he could be trusted. "Don't forget to destroy the paper," he cautioned.

The criminal smiled and slipped the paper into his pocket. "Thank you, Old Wong."

Moments later, a guard called off the break. The work unit lined up and resumed harvesting weeds. Mr. Wong, remembering his recent beating, struggled to keep several steps ahead of the others. As the inmates walked back to the compound, Mr. Wong wished the guards would compliment him for doing his job well. When he did something right, no one noticed, but if he slacked off even once, he was punished. Mr. Wong could forgive the guard, but forgiving and forgetting are different concepts.

From time to time, the prisoners received mail. This day, when he entered his niche, Mr. Wong found a package from Pastor Charlie Chu. Inside were a jacket and a letter with ten renminbi enclosed. The letter apologized that jackets were difficult to buy in Shanghai since liberation. Many of the church members had been imprisoned for reeducation, making it very hard to find a coat for him. The pastor regretted that the jacket wasn't new; a church elder had sent his own spare coat. He hoped it was the right size.

Mr. Wong knew the money would come in handy the next time he took a trip into town. In spite of the apparent desolation of their surroundings, there was a small town a few miles away, on the other side of a mountain, and occasionally a few prisoners were allowed to go into town with the guards.

The occasional mail that the prisoners received also came through this town. From time to time, Mr. Wong received precious letters from his children. These letters brought great courage to his heart, especially as he read of their continuing faithfulness to Jesus. The letters told how the church members helped the children enough that they had the food and clothes they needed to survive. Mr. Wong cherished every letter. He kept them all in his suitcase and read them often. Whenever possible, he also wrote to the children, but he was careful not to say too much about the hardships he was enduring.

Mr. Wong tucked the money from this latest package into his suitcase and thanked God for the thoughtfulness of the church members. He knew they had sacrificed to send him his gift.

One of the other prisoners saw the money that Mr. Wong had received in the package. "Who sent you money?" he asked.

"Some friends from my church in Shanghai," Mr. Wong replied with a smile. He felt happy to be able to give credit to people who loved His Friend Jesus the way he did.

"Your church members must be wonderful people," the other prisoner said in amazement. "How can they afford to send you ten renminbi when salaries are so low?" Mr. Wong felt happy that some prisoners viewed his church positively, and he hoped that they'd believe in his Friend Jesus.

Mr. Wong especially enjoyed *xuxi,* the lunch breaks on workdays, when he had a measure of privacy out on the rolling hills to study pages from the Bible. These moments gave him strength to live a Christian example for one more day.

During one of these lunch breaks, the prisoner to whom he'd given the First Regulation approached him. "Old Wong, listen to this: 'You shall have no other gods before me.' "

Mr. Wong beamed and scribbled down the Second Regulation on a piece of toilet paper and handed it to his fellow prisoner. "Don't forget to destroy the paper! Memorize this Second Regulation. Repeat it to me. Then I'll give you the next one."

The inmate stuck the paper in his pocket. As the work unit lined up for the afternoon's harvesting, Mr. Wong had a merry heart, hoping that inmate might learn to love the Real God. Was this the reason why his Friend had allowed him to come to the hard labor camp?

That evening in his niche, Mr. Wong reread the cherished collection of letters from his children. He felt happy that his daughters were doing well in school and had promised that when they graduated they wouldn't take jobs offered by the government that conflicted with their Sabbath keeping. Their gifts of medicine and moral support strengthened him to brave yet another day in prison.

The quiet ended abruptly when armed guards burst in with the prisoner with whom he'd shared two Regulations.

"Did you give him this?" a guard demanded, holding out a note he'd given the prisoner.

He'd been betrayed. Another prisoner to avoid. Wondering what merit the prisoner had been offered, he replied, "The note's one of the Ten Regulations of Jesus, my Friend."

"These laws are counterrevolutionary! You should be memorizing the sayings of Chairman Mao!" the judas declared.

Knowing he'd broken the prison regulation against proselytizing, and seeing the guns in the guards' hands, Mr. Wong dashed outside, with the guards in hot pursuit. There, he fell to his knees as a terrible memory flashed into his mind. Some time before, a guard's look had encouraged two quarreling prisoners to fight to the death. When the victor arose triumphant, expecting a reward, he was accused of murder. The prisoner protested,

"You told me to kill him. I followed orders!" Moments later a bullet penetrated his skull. Two prisoners had died without trial.

Folding his hands, Mr. Wong prayed. "I'm willing to die if that's what You want, but I'd rather live to be a witness in prison. Please, don't let me die now!" So intent was he in prayer that he paid no attention to the guards.

After several minutes, he heard a familiar voice, the head of the guards, who had liked the Bible verse "He who doesn't work won't eat!"

"What are you doing, Criminal Wong?" the head guard asked. "Are you praying to your God?"

"I'm talking to Jesus, my Friend, the Son of the Real God, telling Him I'm not ready to die."

"Your reaction seems natural!" the head guard exclaimed. "My grandmother is a Christian, but her behavior made Christianity a joke. You must be a true Christian, Criminal Wong."

At that, the other guards left, leaving Mr. Wong praying until he felt certain all danger had passed. For a time, he was able to witness privately with little fear of repercussion from the guards.

Then the guard whose grandmother had been a Christian completed his term of duty and was transferred out of the labor camp. A new supervisor, named Yen, replaced him. His arrival meant new problems. The weekend rolled around, and Mr. Wong prepared, as usual, to be absent from Sabbath work. He wrote out a request, wondering how Supervisor Yen would react.

Chapter 18

SABBATH IS JUST SATURDAY

Mr. Wong worked faithfully and diligently all week, but on Saturday, when Supervisor Yen called morning roll in the center of the cave, he was absent. The supervisor called his name again. "Is Criminal Wong sick?" The prisoners stood at attention. No one spoke. Growing angry, he demanded, "His request for a day off from work was refused! Why is he absent?"

Still no reply.

Marching up and down the rows of prisoners, the supervisor stopped and glared at the ones who didn't meet his eye. In a loud voice, he barked, "I'll grant merit to the prisoner who knows where Criminal Wong is."

Someone told him.

"In what unit does he work?" Supervisor Yen demanded.

A guard answered, "Team 9." The supervisor ordered all except Team 9 to follow their guards to work. These he ordered to follow him.

They found Mr. Wong in his niche, meditating.

"Your arrogant request for a holiday was denied. Why didn't you report for duty today, Criminal Wong?" Supervisor Yen shouted angrily when he saw Mr. Wong sitting alone. "Your action's disrupted your entire work unit!"

Mr. Wong set aside his medical book. "Other guards have granted me Sabbaths off."

"They were wrong!" the supervisor shot back. "How can I give you a day off?"

"I'm a Seventh-day Adventist."

"I know you worship Jesus." Knowing from the dossiers that Mr. Wong was studious, Supervisor Yen decided to use reason. "I know religions well, and I believe Jesus was a good man." He paced back and forth while the other prisoners listened. "But Western imperialists used Jesus' teachings to change other countries' cultures. Don't you understand that your government, following the will of the people, wants to rid us of Western influence?"

"I thought like you once," Mr. Wong replied. "To me, Christianity was an alien influence. But when I studied the Old and New Testaments myself, I found out differently." Mr. Wong flashed his charming smile. "Now I believe the Bible teaches people the best way to live."

"With so many gods teaching different ways, all claiming to have the truth, it's impossible to know which one's right," Mr. Yen said. Continuing his logical approach, he led the discussion away from religion. "That's why I'm glad we have science."

"Science doesn't reveal truth. It only points in the direction of truth. Real truth is found only in the Word of the Real God. The Testaments teach that I may work six days, but I must rest the seventh day. On that day I can do no work."

"Criminal Wong, you were arrested for many reasons, but partly because you refused to work in your factory on Saturday; the People's Court found you guilty and sent you here for reeducation. Have you learned nothing here? You're still committing the same crimes! What does it take to free you from your superstitious shackles?"

"The government is very kind to spend time reeducating me. I've already learned much from you." Mr. Wong smiled. "But, as a true Christian, I cannot disobey the laws of the Real God."

Frustrated, Supervisor Yen burst out, "You persist in breaking China's laws?"

"Seventh-day Adventists believe it's their duty to obey the government—as long as it doesn't go against God's laws. If I have to sin against your government in order not to sin against God, I choose to break my government's regulations!"

"Criminal Wong, you're in a hard labor camp. In prison you must work. It's your sentence. You have no choice."

"I'll gladly work six days a week, but the seventh day is the Sabbath of the Real God, who created everything, including you and me. I regret that my government's regulation is contrary to the law of God."

Amazed at the firmness and sincerity of Mr. Wong's words, the supervisor determined to break his stubbornness. "I'm sure your so-called Real God would make an exception for criminals in hard labor camps who must work." He shifted his tone to compassion. "We have priests available who could give you an absolution. I'll arrange it for you."

"A priest isn't above God's laws."

Unwilling to lose face in front of the prisoners from Team 9, Supervisor Yen barked, "It's my duty to free you from your religious opiate! There is no god—and you must learn to obey orders. The People's government knows no exception. You'll pay for your counterrevolutionary activities!" Turning to the other prisoners, he commanded, "If you're loyal to Chairman Mao, beat Criminal Wong!"

The inmates in Team 9 took turns kicking Mr. Wong in the ribs, smiting his chest, and slapping his face. They grabbed him, pushed him above ground, and knocked him down. Forcing him to kneel, they tied his hands behind his back. Some threw stones at him. The blows came from everywhere. His outer body felt extreme pain, but inside he felt peace. "Thank You, Jesus," he prayed, "for this opportunity to suffer so that others may know how true Christians behave when treated badly. Please reveal Your great power, if it's to Your glory. Show these unbelievers that You are the Real God."

The frenzied inmates laughed and yelled, "Hit harder! He's calling on his God to stop us!"

Supervisor Yen sent a guard to round up all the other Christians in the camp. When they arrived, Yen barked, "Teach all Christians a lesson!" As Team 9 hit Mr. Wong more severely, the Christians watched helplessly, knowing they'd receive similar punishment if they intervened. The supervisor taunted the other Christians, saying, "Why does he pray to his so-called Real God? Why do you thought criminals pray? Can't you see He can't help you?"

Mr. Wong continued praying.

"If you want to prove that your so-called Real God exists, ask him to stop the prisoners from beating you!" he mocked. Turning to the Team 9 prisoners, he ordered, "Resume beating Criminal Wong for Chairman Mao's sake!"

The prisoners obeyed.

"What's wrong, Criminal Wong?" Supervisor Yen laughed. "How come nothing happened? Is this small group of criminals too strong for your so-called Real God? Is he afraid?"

Mr. Wong made no reply. He didn't pray for the persecution to end but for his family to grow up to be good Christians. He became so involved in prayer that he scarcely felt the blows crashing against him.

"Stop!" Supervisor Yen shouted, and the inmates obeyed. He walked up to Mr. Wong and spoke kindly. "We don't need to hurt you, Criminal Wong. The beating will stop if you agree to work. Are you going to work?"

Mr. Wong closed his eyes and renewed his silent vigil.

"You're such a stubborn coward!" Supervisor Yen yelled. "You're afraid to step out of the darkness that binds you and enter New China. But you'll learn."

"Tie him up!" the supervisor ordered, and the prisoners grabbed the kneeling man and tied his arms to his legs.

Mr. Wong prayed aloud, "My Friend Jesus, I remember that Jacob in his time of trouble wrestled with You until You gave him a blessing. Look kindly on me, a sinner, and send me a blessing. I won't let You go unless You bless both me and my family."

Frustrated, some guards began to finger the triggers on their weapons. "We could easily kill you. The workers in Team 9 could beat you to death, or the guards could shoot you. Why? Because you believe in a god that doesn't exist! Ask your government to bless you, not your god."

Closing his eyes again, Mr. Wong prayed aloud, "Jesus, my Friend, You sacrificed Your life that I might live. If I'm sacrificed today, it will be a small sacrifice compared to Yours. I gladly accept the honor."

"Let me ask you, Criminal Wong," the supervisor interrupted.

"If we were to kill you today, what would be the use of your so-called sacrifice? Nothing—an utter waste. Please, don't follow the path of the Catholic priest who was sentenced to reeducation for fifteen years, but when he refused to change, had to be committed to a second fifteen years. How many seasons does a man live? I hope you wake up before your seasons are over!"

Mr. Wong prayed aloud, "Jesus, I confess my sins. I know that You hold the key to unlock the grave. Make me worthy to be raised in the resurrection when You return."

The supervisor laughed nervously. "Criminal Wong! Refute your religion, and your life will be easy! We're your friends. It's your foolish religion that's your enemy." His tone again became kindly. "We care about you."

Mr. Wong knew he was lying.

"We want you to live," the supervisor continued. "It's my job to purify you, and I can't do that if you're dead. Please understand our actions. You're in prison—that's why we're reeducating you. Learn from your teachers."

Again Mr. Wong prayed that he would be a faithful witness.

"Don't force us to kill you, Criminal Wong," the supervisor threatened. "We'll beat sense into you until you work Saturday." He nodded to the workers in Team 9, who began hitting him fiercely.

Mr. Wong pitied the pain givers and prayed for their forgiveness.

The supervisor screamed, "We don't need forgiveness from your so-called Real God. You need forgiveness from your kind government. Mend your stubborn ways. All will be forgiven you, and we can walk the same road together." The prisoners continued kicking, slapping, and pounding him with their fists.

Mr. Wong prayed again.

"Criminal Wong," the supervisor shouted, "your punishment can end instantly. I can subdue their anger. Your Jesus cannot. Beg me, not your dead god."

As the blows smashed into his face, ribs, and back, Mr. Wong looked at Supervisor Yen. "Your request puts you in the place of God," he said as well as he could with his swollen lips.

"I'm no more of a god than your Friend Jesus. But I am real, and I can help."

Despite his pain, Mr. Wong declared, "I'll worship only the one True God." Then he resumed his prayer for endurance as the beating continued.

"I'll ask you one last time, Criminal Wong. Will you work today?"

Though his body was covered with bruises and he longed for the beating to end, Mr. Wong knew that if he gave in now, he would never have the Sabbath off again. Boldly he replied, though every syllable caused intense pain, "I cannot work on God's Sabbath!"

The supervisor sighed. "Some day, Criminal Wong, you'll wake up and realize that your Sabbath is only Saturday, just another day."

The beating continued but at a subdued rate. The prisoners were tired and eager to eat. The trial had been excruciatingly painful, but Mr. Wong—and his Friend Jesus—had won a great victory. The supervisor hadn't forced him to work on the Sabbath!

The next Sabbath the persecution was repeated. The supervisor's words varied, but the blows hurt as much. The following week was almost the same, and this continued for many weeks. But Mr. Wong never broke the Sabbath, despite the weekly beatings. After six months, the beatings stopped and he was allowed to worship his Real God as he saw fit.

Chapter 19

"PLEASE, DON'T MAKE HIM DIE!"

Fifteen minutes by foot from the prison compound was a mill that ground highland barley into flour for bread. The prisoners who were privileged to work there found it a respite from the pressure of the labor camp.

Mr. Wong and an inmate-physician by the name of Lai made an odd pair—the short doctor, fine-featured and dark-skinned, compared to tall Mr. Wong, large-boned and fair-skinned. No guard stood watch over them, so while they worked, they could talk candidly. Upon arrival, they poured highland barley into the grindstone, took their places on either side, placed their hands on a rod that penetrated the grindstone, and began circling it.

Thinking some of the doctor's words made no sense or sounded strange, Mr. Wong asked, "Dr. Lai, are you a Guangdong person?"

"I'm from Canton." Canton is the Cantonese name for the capital of Guangdong Province. In Mandarin, the language spoken by the prisoners, the city of Canton is called "Guangzhou."

"I thought you were from the south," Mr. Wong said with a smile.

"My Mandarin is so poor!" the doctor replied humbly. "Cantonese has eight tones, while Mandarin has only four. I mix up my tones, making words with vastly different meanings. Sometimes I switch languages. If no one understands, I write the character on my hand with my finger." He laughed. "It's a good thing we Chinese all *read* the same language."

The two circled for a while without speaking.

"You're a political prisoner—Christian—aren't you, Old Wong?" Dr. Lai broke the silence. "What's your crime?"

The question was music to Mr. Wong's ears. "My crime is telling others of Jesus, my Friend, and His Ten Regulations." He paused to reload the mill. Circling again, he added, "I talk of signs of the world's end and Jesus' imminent return."

"So they arrested you for proselytizing?"

"Right. What brought you here?"

"I'm a patriotic Chinese who returned to the motherland after completing medical studies abroad. I thought I'd be welcomed in the New China. Wrong! When Chairman Mao instigated his campaign to let a Hundred Flowers Bloom, I believed in his sincerity and advised the government on how to improve. Big mistake. China didn't trust my foreign education, so intellectuals like me, who could really help New China, must waste their days in hard labor camps."

"Too bad," Mr. Wong sympathized. They poured more grain on the grindstone.

"Yes," the doctor continued. "Working at this mill, I feel like my life is a waste, but when I ease the misery of sick inmates, I'm glad."

"You're a good man, Dr. Lai," Mr. Wong said as they stored the flour and filled the grindstone again. "Have you ever studied the Old and New Testaments?"

"I've read them casually," the doctor replied. After a moment, he added, "It seems you could teach me much."

"Do you know the Ten Regulations?"

"What are they?"

"May I teach you the Ten Regulations one by one? Will you repeat them after me until you can say them by memory?"

The doctor consented. "Anything to take the monotony out of rotating this grindstone!"

Mr. Wong explained the meaning of each of the Ten Commandments, adding information from his long-distance study. Each time, he quoted scriptural texts for verification and asked the doctor to memorize them.

"How did you learn all this?"

"Once I was a sniper and a gambler who often quarreled with my two wives over money," Mr. Wong said. "But one day I found two black books with golden edges in a pharmacy. As I studied them, I fell in love with God's Son, my Friend Jesus. I accepted Him as my Saviour. The Real God transformed me into a devoted husband of one wife. I became a church deacon. I love Him so much I tell others that my Friend is coming soon to end the troubles of this world and take those who love Him and keep the Ten Regulations to live with Him in heaven forever."

Dr. Lai worked quietly, seemingly lost in thought. "This makes good sense. I've needed a change in my life. I want to have this Jesus as my Friend too."

Mr. Wong's heart pounded with joy. "May I tell my Friend Jesus of your decision?"

Dr. Lai smiled his consent. As they walked in circles, Mr. Wong, talking to the Real God, felt He must have smiled too. His time in hard labor was now worthwhile. Perhaps his Friend had sent him to Tsinghai just to meet Dr. Lai.

One morning as the prisoners were lining up to work, one of the guards approached Mr. Wong. "Come with me!" he ordered.

Mr. Wong followed the guard, hoping that he was being taken to a different work assignment rather than to another torture session for his faith. The guard led the way back into the burrow and into a dimly lighted niche, where a man whom Mr. Wong recognized as Dr. Lai attended to bony prisoners lying on blankets. Mr. Wong knew that this particular niche had been reserved as a sort of makeshift hospital for the sickest of the sick. From time to time in the past, he had worked here himself, but the number of patients seemed greatly increased now.

The guard turned around and faced Mr. Wong. "Physician-inmate Lai needs an assistant," he explained. Turning to the doctor, he said, "Criminal Wong will join your work unit today." The guard left the two alone with the sick prisoners.

Though Mr. Wong was delighted to be assigned to work with Dr. Lai, he was dismayed by the large number of wasted bodies whose skin barely covered their bones. "It's the drought," Dr.

Lai explained. "Not enough food. Too much hard work. Many got sick from gobbling up the guards' dung. That's why cleaning the guards' toilet is so popular! Some will live, but it's only a matter of time before the others will be carried away, two at a time, hanging from an inmate's shoulder holder, most of them weighing less than thirty kilos. Starved to death, but I can't write that in the records."

"Why can't you tell the truth?" Mr. Wong felt worried about his new convert.

"The guards got upset the first time I recorded starvation from malnutrition. They said my statement was too subjective and told me to write that I injected the inmate with 3,000 cc of grape sugar at mealtimes, adding that the patient died and nothing could be done."

"Surely some will be fortunate."

The doctor concurred.

"What, besides praying, can we do for the luckier ones?" Mr. Wong asked.

"Feed them emergency rations and hope. If we feed them solid food, they'll die, but if we don't give them some nutrition, they'll die, so we give them watered-down soup. Most are too weak to eat alone, so you'll have to feed them."

He moved to another prisoner. "This is Lee Man Kai. He's not sick, just tired. He asked me to declare him ill so he wouldn't have to work today. If I write a note saying someone's sick, the guards usually believe me. In return, I let Old Lee help me treat the patients when the guards aren't looking. Someday, if you need a rest, I may do the favor for you, Old Wong! Just ask!"

The cooks brought in the rations for the patients. "Let's get busy," Dr. Lai said. He handed some bowls to Mr. Wong and Lee Man Kai, which they filled with watered-down soup. With a bowl in one hand and a spoon in the other, each assistant squatted beside the healthier inmates one at a time and helped them eat their rations. Dr. Lai worked on the other side of the niche.

Lee Man Kai joined Mr. Wong. "Old Wong, you're a Christian, aren't you? Tell me about God."

"I can teach you His Ten Regulations." Mr. Wong placed a spoon in a prisoner's mouth and waited for him to swallow. "Or

I can tell you the signs that indicate the end of the world and Jesus' soon return."

"You're a good man, Old Wong." Lee Man Kai fetched a bowl of soup for the next patient. As he passed Mr. Wong, he added quietly, "I want to learn about the Old and New Testaments."

When the bowl in his hand was empty, Mr. Wong went to fill it. He wondered, Was Old Lee sincere? Yet despite the possibility of betrayal, he must speak for his Friend. He wrote down the First Regulation on a strip of toilet paper. When he thought no one was looking, he handed it to Lee Man Kai. "On the paper is the First Regulation," he said. "Memorize it, and throw the paper away. When you can quote it to me, I'll give you the next one."

The next day Lee Man Kai didn't show up in the hospital niche, so Mr. Wong assisted Dr. Lai alone. About a week later, Mr. Lee returned. As Mr. Wong poured soup into a bowl, beyond the ears of the patients, Inmate Lee spoke softly: "You shall have no other gods before Me!"

Excited, Mr. Wong wrote down the Second Regulation on toilet paper and handed it to Mr. Lee with the same instructions. Gratefully placing the gift in his pocket, Mr. Lee continued feeding patients. Mr. Wong hoped Old Lee would become his second convert.

Mr. Wong assisted Dr. Lai day after day during the drought. Their friendship grew rapidly, for they had a common Friend in Jesus. Dr. Lai always ensured that Mr. Wong had extra servings of steamed rolls, saying, "I like you, Old Wong. You're a good worker. I want you to live. You can't survive on prison rations, so you're lucky to have me as a friend."

"The Real God must have sent you," Mr. Wong said as he ate his additional roll.

"Someday, Old Wong, the drought will end," the doctor predicted, "and the guards will take you back to the fields. When that day comes, I'll visit your team and call to you." He looked warily around the room, then whispered, "When you see me, Old Wong, come to the exact spot where I stand, and you'll find a gift. Don't forget what I just said because I won't say it again."

"I'll remember," Mr. Wong answered, feeling grateful toward

both his friend in camp and his Friend Jesus for his good fortune.

Mr. Wong rejoiced that some patients lived, but he felt sad when others died. He learned the names of those who lived and gave them equal attention. As he cared for them, he longed to give them hope that only the Real God can give a dying man. When they lay suffering or dying, he sat close to them, held their hands, and asked them if they knew his Friend Jesus. Some were interested; others not.

Lee Man Kai frequented the sick ward, pretending to be ill and doing odd jobs for Dr. Lai. "Old Wong," he said one day as they were filling bowls, "tell me more about God."

"Have you memorized the Second Regulation, Old Lee?"

Dutifully, Inmate Lee quoted the Second Regulation. Pleased that Mr. Lee showed an interest, Mr. Wong wrote out the Third Regulation, handing it to him with his usual instructions. Lee Man Kai smiled as he took the text and stuck it in his pocket.

Later, as Mr. Wong lighted candles in the hospital niche, a guard entered. "Criminal Wong, come with me into the weed fields to harvest."

Dr. Lai's prediction had come true.

Exercising his privilege as a physician-inmate, Dr. Lai visited the man who prepared food, taking extra servings of steamed rolls. No one said anything, for they assumed the rolls were for the ailing. Nobody suspected his secret plan, which soon became a daily routine. Wrapping the rolls in the camp's typical hefty toilet paper, the doctor slipped them into his coat pocket. He left the burrow, walked past the sentry's mound in the middle of the prison grounds, and exited the prison gate. As he walked the rolling plain, Dr. Lai enjoyed his freedom to inspect for injuries and illnesses. This privilege enabled him to preserve his strength.

His route led him to the fields where Mr. Wong's unit harvested weeds. Standing in the distance, he watched the bent-over workers swinging their sickles and stuffing their baskets. Drawing nearer, he shouted, "Work hard, Old Wong!" He watched proudly as Mr. Wong surged ahead of the rest of his team. Of all the prisoners, none worked harder. The doctor feared that without proper food, Mr. Wong wouldn't survive.

Admiringly, Dr. Lai called out even louder, "Work hard, Old Wong!" He saw Mr. Wong look in his direction. Satisfied that his friend had memorized his position, the doctor initiated his secret plan. Squatting as if to fulfill a call of nature, he hid the steamed rolls in the vegetation. He stood and called again, "Work hard, Old Wong!" and went away.

When he thought it appropriate, Mr. Wong set down his sickle and basket, walked up to the team leader, and announced, "I need to make water."

With permission, he walked toward the place where the doctor had called his name. If he returned quickly, no questions would be asked. Finding the exact spot, Mr. Wong squatted. Seeing the toilet paper nearby, he unwrapped the rolls, quickly devoured them, and returned to harvesting weeds, grateful for Dr. Lai's kindness. He hoped their friendship would never cause the doctor any trouble.

One morning in 1960, before the sun had risen, the prisoners lined up for their regular morning call and exercises on the ground atop their cave. Shivering as the warden called the roll, they waited for the exercises that would get their blood circulating. But instead of starting the exercises, when the roll call was completed, the warden called, "Criminal Glorious Country Wong." He paused and beckoned Mr. Wong to come.

Mr. Wong broke ranks and stood in front of the warden. The warden said, "You're handsome, Criminal Wong. I admire your charm."

"Thank you," Mr. Wong said modestly. "I'm not handsome."

The warden smiled kindly. "I like you, and I think you're a good man, so I want to help you."

Mr. Wong suspected a trick but smiled courteously, saying, "Thank you."

"Don't thank me yet, Criminal Wong," the warden said with typical Chinese humility. "I'm afraid I can't do much for you, but I'll do the best I can." Checking the dossiers, he stated, "You're working in Team 9. If I were you, I wouldn't want to work on that team. It's the worst in the camp. You're far too good a worker to be placed on that team."

"I'm not afraid of hard work and good exercise. He who does not work cannot eat!" Mr. Wong felt his hard work made him healthier than the other prisoners.

The warden placed his arm around Mr. Wong's neck in a gesture of camaraderie. "I'd like to reassign you to Team 5."

"I'll work wherever you assign me." Mr. Wong's warm, deep-set eyes sparkled.

"You realize my plan's special. I'm being very kind to you, Criminal Wong. If I reassign you to Team 5, I'll need cooperation on your part."

"What do you want me to do?" Mr. Wong smiled, his suspicions mounting.

"One thing: Give up your God!" The warden looked out at the lines of prisoners. "Look, Criminal Wong. All the prisoners stand before you, eager to start their exercises, but they await your answer. Criminal Wong, my one request is an easy one. Just tell me—" he gestured toward the line, "and them—that you'll give up your God."

Silence reigned. Mr. Wong prayed for guidance and strength. The warden's offer was incredible. Did he take him for a fool? Full compliance would still leave him in the labor camp. He could be reassigned to Team 9 without notice. Before he answered, he thanked his Friend for another opportunity to witness. In a clear voice, he proclaimed, "The Scriptures say that if anyone denies the Real God before men, Jesus will deny him before His Father in heaven." As he looked over the lineup of prisoners, he longed to teach them truth. "I cannot, like Peter, deny my Friend Jesus. Instead, I openly declare that Jesus is my only trust!"

"You stubborn fool! Don't you realize you're on the brink of a precipice? Rein in your stubborn horse!" The warden's politeness turned to rage. "What gall to shun my kind offer! Your arrogance, Criminal Wong, must be punished!"

The guards, incensed by Mr. Wong's reply, raised their fists high and shouted, "Criminal Wong, rein in your arrogant, stubborn horse! Surrender your pride, or suffer the consequences."

When the shouts subsided, the warden asked, "Criminal Wong, did you hear what they said?"

Mr. Wong made no reply but prayed inwardly for courage to withstand the persecution he knew was coming.

"Guards!" the warden ordered, "choose your strongest inmates! Retrain this counterrevolutionary insurgent."

Obediently the guards selected fifty strong prisoners and brought them to the front. "Beat this radical!" they yelled. "Kick him until he's brave enough to give up his God!"

Immediately, the fifty men began striking Mr. Wong's body with their fists and feet and slapping his cheeks.

Among the prisoners witnessing Mr. Wong's punishment were a Catholic priest and Dr. Lai. The priest, deeply troubled, knew that he could be the next victim. He asked himself if he were ready to be loyal to God like Old Wong. With every blow against Mr. Wong's body, both priest and doctor winced, though neither dared reflect their true emotions on their faces. They saw his face redden and grow puffy and heard the inmates chant with each blow, "Repent! Repent! Repent!"

Would they beat him to death? The priest remembered what Jesus said about other cheeks and marveled at the Protestant's ability to remain calm. The doctor saw a blow that threw Mr. Wong's head backward, causing him to fall to the ground and roll in agony.

"Stop!" the warden commanded. Gently, he lifted Mr. Wong to his feet and placed his arm around his shoulder to steady him. The doctor felt incensed that the first thing Mr. Wong would see when he came around would be the face of a smiling tiger.

"I'm your friend, Criminal Wong," the doctor and priest heard the warden lie. "I don't like to see you punished, so I ordered them to stop!" Both doctor and priest noted that he neglected to mention who had ordered the persecution to start. Would the smiling tiger pounce again?

When Mr. Wong opened his mouth, his jaw hurt, but he managed to murmur, "You're very kind to me."

"You understand," the warden explained, "it's because you're so stubborn that the inmates punish you! The beatings will stop if you will disavow your phony Lord. It's that easy! I'll transfer you from Team 9 to Team 5 because I like you."

Mr. Wong leaned heavily against the warden and painfully mustered a smile. "I know you mean to be good to me. If I could follow your wishes, I would. But in this case, I must remain firm."

"I'm your teacher. It's your duty to learn from me." The warden sounded sincere. "Will you renounce your God for me? Don't be afraid!"

"Why do you think I'm afraid?" Mr. Wong asked. "I'm a brave man! You have no idea the courage it takes to stand here and take the inmates' beatings in silence," Mr. Wong replied.

"Your life is not a game! Stop and think. If you lay your stubborn religious thoughts aside, we could walk down the same path joyously and proudly together as friends!"

Mr. Wong wondered why the warden smiled more warmly when he lied.

"I care about you. Be born again—start anew!"

"Warden, I was born again when I met my Friend Jesus. I tell you, I'm not afraid to honor the Real God."

The warden removed his arm from around Mr. Wong's shoulder. His eyes glared with renewed anger. "Criminal Wong hasn't learned his lesson!" he shouted toward the lineup as he stepped away. Looking at the selected persecution party, he ordered, "Punish him until he does learn!" Instantly, the fifty resumed pounding Mr. Wong's chest, slapping his face and kicking his waist and legs. Already weakened by the first beating, each blow felt more painful as it landed on bruises from the previous pounding. His swollen face became like raw meat, but he stood his ground.

As the pelting continued, the pain tempted him to deny Jesus, like Peter. Surely his Friend would forgive, and God would understand. Hadn't Jesus forgiven Peter and later chosen him to become a great leader? What made him think he was any better than Peter? Why should he tolerate this cruelty? His police training told him to resist, but when Peter cut off Malchus's ear, Jesus replaced it. In his anguish, Mr. Wong longed to follow the example of Jesus, who had reluctantly drunk His cup of death for every person, including himself. The intense suffering tempted him to renounce his Friend.

Suddenly, Mr. Wong remembered letters from his second daughter, Lin, encouraging him to be strong. How could he write back saying he'd been untrue? He couldn't disappoint her! For her sake, he'd live and die a good example. Those fifty prisoners could injure his body, but they couldn't lay a finger on his soul.

With his inner struggle resolved, he calmly suffered in silence. His confidence heightened their anger, causing them to strike harder and to shout more fiercely, "Repent! Repent!" They struck Mr. Wong more frequently until his nerves felt numb. "Renounce your God, you no-good person!" shouted an inmate as he struck an unusually heavy blow that knocked Mr. Wong to the ground unconscious.

"Stop!" Dr. Lai could no longer contain his emotions. "Please, don't make him die!" The priest admired the doctor, wishing he had the courage to protest.

The persecution party paused, and Mr. Wong sat up feebly.

"Who said that?" the warden demanded as he walked along the line of prisoners, eyeing them with fierce looks. When he came to the priest, he stared suspiciously at him. The priest squirmed at the scrutiny. Next, the warden looked at Dr. Lai.

"I did," the doctor confessed.

"Who gave you permission to give orders?"

"No one."

"Why did you order them to stop?"

"I'm a doctor. I feared they'd kill Prisoner Wong."

The warden laughed sickeningly. "This is conspiracy!" He marched over to where Mr. Wong sat sprawled on the ground, looked down at him contemptuously, and spat near his face. "You and Dr. Lai planned this! Criminal Wong, you forget that your government is merciful. The beatings stop when you obey! To seek out an inmate for help and not your government is a great sin!"

Dr. Lai hoped he hadn't unwittingly brought more suffering upon Mr. Wong. His outburst had been spontaneous, but he knew he could never convince the warden, especially since he and Mr. Wong were known to be good friends. "Are you worried about Criminal Wong's health?" the warden demanded.

"I feared you might kill him."

"Why do you care?"

"I'm a doctor. From my years of medical experience, I know his injuries are severe."

Instantly, as if on cue, the persecution party dashed over to Dr. Lai and started beating him instead of Mr. Wong. They knocked him to the ground, kicking and pounding him. "That's enough!" the guard ordered, and the prisoners stopped.

"Criminal Wong sought you out to defend him!" the warden sneered. "Your appeal is futile. Prisoners, beat Criminal Wong more severely. Teach him not to appeal to fellow inmates. Teach physician-inmate Lai to learn tranquility!" Now the fifty inmates kicked and beat Mr. Wong harder and shouted even louder, "Repent! Renounce your God!"

"Dr. Lai, you misunderstood my actions," the warden shouted over the din. "It's my job to remove the bourgeois liberalism that the People disapprove. I must rid the masses of their feudal ideas of materialism, superstition, capitalism, and religion. Nothing you say, Dr. Lai, can change the outcome. Criminal Wong has earned his grief. In his cowardice, he clings to religion. This beating is retribution for his sin!"

Dr. Lai said nothing.

When the beating wound down at last, Mr. Wong felt especially appreciative of the man who had been willing to protest at such personal risk. Dr. Lai did pay a price for his courage, for he was forbidden to practice medicine and was forced into hard labor. Later, both the Catholic priest and Dr. Lai were transferred to another prison compound. The doctor and Mr. Wong never saw each other again, but Dr. Lai was never far away in Mr. Wong's thoughts.

With no doctor in the camp, the guards often asked Mr. Wong to tend the sick, giving him additional opportunities to teach Lee Man Kai about his Friend Jesus and the Ten Regulations. He ardently hoped that Lee Man Kai was genuinely interested and not a judas.

Chapter 20

AN ANGEL UNTIED THE KNOT

One day during the coldest part of the winter in 1961, a jailer burst into the prison hospital niche where Mr. Wong was working. "Criminal Wong, come with me!"

Mr. Wong wondered, *Will I be assigned to a new post, or am I in for more punishment?* He followed the jailer into a larger niche.

Minutes later, Lee Man Kai was escorted in. "Criminal Wong," the jailer scolded, "we know you've been explaining superstitious beliefs."

So Lee Man Kai was a judas too, hoping to receive merit or a reduced prison term.

"Criminal Lee gave us this." The jailer handed Mr. Wong the toilet paper—evidence of betrayal. "You gave this to Criminal Lee, didn't you?"

"Yes, I wrote out scriptural texts for him. This is one of the Ten Regulations."

"Stop telling bourgeois liberalistic stories about the Real God," the jailer yelled. "Teach Chairman Mao's sayings, not Jesus' fables!"

Mr. Wong looked straight into the jailer's eyes. "Lonely prisoners need to know the Word of Jesus."

The jailer glared back. "You're in prison for your superstitious activities." Angrily, he bound Mr. Wong and ordered Lee Man Kai to beat him. As Inmate Lee hit him, the jailer sneered, "We have rules about religion. You must obey, Criminal Wong!"

"I'm sorry your rules go against the laws of Jesus, my Friend, who is the Son of the Real God." Mr. Wong spoke solemnly. "I'll follow Peter's example when the Jewish Sanhedrin told him to stop talking about Jesus. Peter chose to obey God's laws rather than people's."

Suddenly, Lee Man Kai's face lighted up. Eagerly, he stepped up to the jailer, saying conspiratorially, "Other people tied Criminal Wong, but he could still move. If I bind somebody, he can't move unless I release him! I have a special knot," he bragged, pressing for favor. "I call it my Lee Man Kai knot. No one can untie it but me! Let me bind Criminal Wong with it. I promise, you won't be disappointed."

An impish grin broke across the jailer's face, indicating he approved of the plan to tie up the troublesome Mr. Wong. Anything to persuade him to change. "Do as you like, Criminal Lee. What's your plan?"

"Take him out into the cold and tie him to a post," Inmate Lee urged. When the jailer consented, Mr. Lee doffed a hat and coat and fashioned his tightest knot around Mr. Wong's wrists. The pressure stopped the circulation, turning Mr. Wong's fingers slightly blue. Several inmates grabbed Mr. Wong roughly and followed Lee Man Kai, who had a coil of rope draped over his shoulder. The group dragged Mr. Wong outside the burrow. The cold air took Mr. Wong's breath away. A light snow was falling. Mr. Wong was glad that he had worn heavier clothes that day.

When they reached the outer perimeter of the prison grounds, they dropped Mr. Wong near a post. A stiff, cold wind was blowing as Lee Man Kai strapped Mr. Wong to the post. "I, Lee Man Kai, tied you up today with my tightest knots," he scoffed. "Tomorrow we'll see if your God can save you. You not only have my Lee Man Kai knot to bind you, but the Liberation Army will watch you all night. You must remain motionless. If you so much as move a muscle, a soldier will shoot you immediately!" Lee Man Kai obviously enjoyed his moment of power.

One soldier remained to guard Mr. Wong. Tsinghai's strong north wind and swirling snow dropped the temperature to thirty-eight degrees below zero Celsius. Their breath crackled as it froze before their faces. Eventually, the shivering soldier could endure the cold no longer and walked toward the guard-house. Mr. Wong guessed the soldier had reasoned that they needn't both perish. He watched the soldier struggle laboriously against the wind, staggering back toward warmth and safety.

By midnight, Mr. Wong had difficulty breathing the frigid air. His thick clothes could keep him warm through the night when he slept in the cave, but outside in the swift breeze he felt the cold set in, and he knew he'd soon be frostbitten and freeze to death.

He turned to Jesus. "My Friend, I know You're the Real God. I know that You were crucified for me so I could be saved. I'm willing to be a martyr for You if it's Your will, but I don't think now is the right time. I'd rather die for You when I can give You more glory."

Suddenly, he felt a presence behind him. The next thing he knew, the knots were loose. Mr. Wong wriggled his way out of the rope. He was free! Immediately, he tended to business, relieving his bladder. Then he exercised to stay warm.

All through the long night, Mr. Wong jumped up and down and ran circles around the post. Sometimes he even ventured a few yards away from the post.

And all through the night, he prayed. He prayed that Jesus would keep the guards from seeing him untied, and he prayed that Jesus would keep him strong to endure whatever persecution might lie in the future.

Sometimes, when he felt warm enough to stand the cold for a while, Mr. Wong sat against the post in the same position the guard had left him so that in case one of the guards happened to see him it would look like he was still tied up. But as soon as the cold penetrated his body again, he stood up to exercise. The hours seemed to drag by as Mr. Wong alternated between exercising and resting against the post.

Finally, he saw the sky begin to lighten in the east, and he knew that his torture was nearing its end. Then, as the sun began to rise, he realized that he had another problem. When the guards returned and found him loose, they would accuse someone in the camp of coming to his aid, and they might hurt or kill his supposed benefactor. Furthermore, the accused would very likely be a prisoner who had enjoyed talking about his Friend Jesus. He didn't wish to cause grief to those who showed an interest in the Real God, so he sat down against the post and retied his ankles. But tying his wrists behind his back posed a problem. He needed an extra pair of hands! There seemed no human solution.

He prayed again, "Lord, You sent my guardian angel to untie me. Please send him back to tie me up again!" Immediately he felt the ropes tighten around his hands. He was held fast to the post. A few moments later he heard a guard approaching.

The guard came around in front of Mr. Wong, leaned over, and looked in his face. Mr. Wong smiled. "Good morning!" he said.

The guard gasped, and his face turned white. "You're alive!" he exclaimed. "This can't be. You're supposed to be frozen to death!" He went around to the other side of the post and felt Mr. Wong's hands. "Your hands are warm!" he exclaimed. "They're supposed to be blocks of ice!"

The guard tried untying Mr. Wong's hands, but he had trouble with the knot, so he came around in front and untied his feet first. In just a few seconds, Mr. Wong's feet were free. The guard then returned to the rope around Mr. Wong's hands, but the knot was so tight that he could not untie it. Half an hour later, Mr. Wong finally felt the rope fall from his wrists! He couldn't help thinking that his guardian angel either didn't know his own strength, or he had a delightful sense of humor.

The guard said nothing as they walked back toward the main part of the compound, and Mr. Wong sensed that he had a sense of awe, almost of reverence.

The guard led Mr. Wong up to a fire, around which a group of guards sat warming themselves. Everyone started talking at once the moment they saw Mr. Wong. They asked the guard why his prisoner was not frozen to death, and they asked Mr. Wong how he had survived the night. Mr. Wong's guard found a place for him near the fire where he could enjoy the most heat and breathe in the least smoke. Mr. Wong could scarcely remember when he had been treated so kindly by a guard!

As he warmed his hands and feet near the fire, Mr. Wong

sent a prayer toward heaven. "Thank You, God, for allowing me to experience this miracle. Your angel untied Lee Man Kai's invincible knot. The guards didn't expect me to survive the night. That precious miracle has given me the confidence to believe You will protect me and assist me through any difficulty."

As the sun rose, so did the prisoners. Mr. Wong watched them drag themselves out of the cave into the bitter cold. They gravitated toward the warmth of the campfire. Not certain whether they could trust their eyes, the prisoners formed a circle around Mr. Wong and stared at him without a word. One touched Mr. Wong's wrists to be certain he wasn't an apparition. Mr. Wong knew they wondered how he had survived a night in the cold. He thanked God, feeling certain that soon they would ask him about his Friend, the Real God, who he felt had indeed saved him.

Some tired of staring and returned to their niches. Lee Man Kai, who had bragged so loudly about his famous knot, was conspicuously silent. As they talked among themselves, Mr. Wong heard them refer to him as the "Man Who Couldn't Be Killed." For quite some time, both guards and prisoners left him alone, until new guards were assigned to the hard labor camp.

Chapter 21

"SAY THE TEN REGULATIONS"

Round and round Mr. Wong and Choi Gong-ding went, turning a large grindstone that crushed highland barley. More monotonous than strenuous, the work at the mill afforded an opportunity for Mr. Wong to talk one-on-one with prisoners about his Friend Jesus and the Ten Regulations. Remembering his success with Dr. Lai, he hoped he could witness to Inmate Choi.

As they toiled, Choi Gong-ding seemed more thoughtful than usual. What was going on in his mind? Mr. Wong wondered. Eventually, Mr. Choi revealed his concern. "My mother is a Christian, Old Wong. I'd like to learn more about the Bible and become a Christian like you."

Overjoyed, Mr. Wong replied, "Do you know the Ten Regulations?"

"What are they?"

"Would you like to hear a story?"

"I love stories!"

As the two continued to rotate the millstone, Mr. Wong told how Moses hiked up Mount Sinai to receive the stone tablets on which the Real God had carved the Ten Regulations with His own finger. When Moses came down and saw the people dancing around a golden idol shaped like a calf, he had, in righteous indignation, lifted the tablets over his head and cast them down, shattering them into tiny pieces.

"Why did Moses break a gift from God?" Inmate Choi asked.

Mr. Wong smiled. "All of us have rebelled against those Regulations, just as the people at the foot of Mount Sinai did. When

Moses threw down the stones, breaking them into little bits, it meant that God's people had broken their promise to obey the Regulations of the Real God."

Mr. Wong emptied the ground barley and reloaded the mill. Tempted to supplement his diet with a handful of the grain, he remembered the guard's warning that "any offender taking extra grain will be shot." The rule seemed ridiculous, for he felt worthy of the food as a laborer. Though he might be able to eat some extra barley unnoticed by a guard, he wanted to be an example to his partner. Feeling the ache in his stomach, he put the thought from his mind and gripped the rod. As they resumed circling the millstone, Mr. Wong said, "One of those Ten Regulations explains why I won't work on Sabbath." Delighted that a fellow inmate seemed interested, he prayed silently that Choi Gong-ding would discern truth, understand it, and persevere.

"What are the Ten Regulations?"

Choi Gong-ding had asked what Mr. Wong longed to hear. He recited them from memory and asked Inmate Choi to repeat them after him. Mr. Choi happily complied until he, too, could say all ten by heart. On future occasions, the two men continued studying the Old and New Testaments. Mr. Wong supplied additional verses to memorize until Mr. Choi understood Christianity.

"Old Wong," Inmate Choi said one day as they walked around the grindstone, "I've decided I want Jesus for my Friend. As His friend, I don't want to do anything to displease Him, so I'm asking Him to help me refrain from breaking His Ten Regulations. Do you think He'll do that for me?"

Hearing those words, Mr. Wong felt that his time in prison was doubly well spent. First the doctor had accepted Christ, and now a Christian mother's dreams had come true. Smiling with inner joy, he assured Choi Gong-ding, "Heaven enjoys double happiness today. I'm sure your Friend Jesus will happily help you. But you must make an effort too." Then he cautioned, "Old Choi, don't forget, Jesus never promised that following Him would be easy. From now on, you'll have to take up the sword and fight."

"You've taught me already, Old Wong," Mr. Choi replied as he poured highland barley into the millstone. "I've weighed every-thing carefully."

Later in 1962, when Mr. Wong and three hundred other pris-oners lined up in the cave for morning roll call and exercises, a guard grabbed one of the prisoners and pushed him to the front beside the supervisor. Mr. Wong's heart sank as he recognized his friend, Choi Gong-ding. Had he, too, become a judas?

Suddenly, someone jerked Mr. Wong from behind and roughly escorted him to the front beside Inmate Choi. The three hun-dred pale, puffy-faced prisoners stared blankly at them. Guards called up two of the heftier inmates and directed them to stand on either side of Mr. Wong and Mr. Choi. Immediately, these prisoners shoved Wong's and Choi's heads downward and held them.

"Criminal Wong," the supervisor barked, "did you think you could do anything without us knowing?"

"No."

"Did you think you could talk without us overhearing?"

Mr. Wong made no reply.

"Criminal Choi!" The big prisoner at Choi's side yanked his hair. "Confess your conversation with Criminal Wong!"

"He taught me the Ten Regulations," Inmate Choi mumbled.

"Speak up, Criminal Choi." The hefty inmate holding Mr. Choi's head looked in the direction of the guards and, seeing a slight smile of approval on the guard's face, smacked the back of his head. "Tell everybody what he told you!"

Mr. Wong felt deeply pained to see his friend suffer, knowing he didn't want to confess. Would the torture be too much for him to endure? As he watched Inmate Choi's torment, he prayed that his friend wouldn't weaken. After a brief, agonizing pause, Choi Gong-ding announced in a loud voice, "Criminal Wong told me about an old man with a long white beard named Moses who climbed up a mountain to talk to the Real God. When Moses met the Real God, he received a gift of two tablets of stone. With His own finger, the Real God had written onto them His Ten Regulations that—"

Interrupting, the supervisor shouted, "Criminal Wong, you've been telling silly Bible stories to Criminal Choi! You forced him to memorize superstitious nonsense. You're breaking the prison rules again. Criminal Choi, you are our witness! Repeat what he told you."

The hefty inmate beside Inmate Choi yanked his head upward. Mr. Wong saw fear in his friend's face, and, pitying him, prayed for him again and again. But Mr. Choi's eyes glazed over as he spoke in a staccato, "I am the Lord your God, who brought you out of the land of Egypt, out of the house of bondage.

"You shall have no other gods before Me.

"You shall not make for yourself a carved image—any likeness of anything that is in heaven above, or that is in the earth beneath, or that is in the water under the earth."

Mr. Wong was amazed that the supervisor would allow Choi to continue reciting the Ten Regulations, but the officer made no move to silence him. Mr. Wong listened, and his friend recited all ten of the Regulations without a single mistake. God had provided an opportunity for the guards and the prisoners to hear every one of them! Mr. Wong's heart sang, in spite of the pain in his scalp from the pressure the prisoner beside him was putting on his hair.

All the prisoners listened silently to Mr. Choi's recitation. An air solemn like a monastery hung over the cave.

The supervisor shattered the silence, shouting, "Criminal Choi has presented evidence before you all by chanting superstitious dogma." Turning, he sneered, "Criminal Wong, we asked him to chant that feudalistic nonsense so the prisoners could know your crime."

But Mr. Wong heard the prisoners murmuring amongst themselves. "I'm a thief. I broke the Seventh Regulation. That's why I'm here." Another said, "I killed a man. I broke the Sixth Regulation. That's why I'm here!" The supervisor's plan had backfired!

Rather than feeling embarrassed or defeated, Mr. Wong felt victorious. He never would have guessed that teaching Mr. Choi would result in this wholesale teaching of the Ten Regulations to all the prisoners—at the instigation of his jailers! Truly his Real God had often used wicked people to spread His truth. Silently, he thanked his Friend Jesus for this unexpected opportunity to witness.

Since his crime had been exposed, would further punishment follow? Mr. Wong wondered. As he worked with his unit that day, he felt pity for Inmate Choi, and he felt apprehension that the government would soon retaliate.

That night, as the prisoners ate in the cave, a guard approached Mr. Wong, pulled out a pair of handcuffs, and snapped them onto his wrists. In a loud voice, he announced, "These handcuffs are your punishment for teaching counterrevolutionary ideas to Criminal Choi and for breaking prison regulations. Every night we'll handcuff you until you comply." Before he left, the guard added, "You're lucky, Criminal Wong, that you work hard; otherwise, we'd handcuff you all day long." The handcuffs were a nuisance, making it difficult to sleep, but Mr. Wong felt that they were a small price to pay for three hundred prisoners to hear the Ten Regulations.

Chapter 22

TRAITOROUS UNCLES

The guard entered Mr. Wong's niche with a letter in his hand. "Your daughters refuse to work for the government if they have to work on Saturdays. They're clinging to their superstition," he scolded. "You should advise them to give up their God and support the Party! Do your fatherly duty, and tell them to read Chairman Mao's sayings!" Solemnly, the guard handed Mr. Wong the letter.

Mr. Wong knew that all mail to prisoners was censored. The guard's reprimand brought joy to his heart. After the guard had left, he tore a strip off the side of the envelope, which the guard had resealed, and drew out the letter. Smiling, he read it, then dug out his collection of short notes the government allowed his children to write him monthly. Taking them out of their envelopes, he reread them. These precious children warmed his heart. In the latest letter, Mei-Mei wrote that she had finished school and had requested work with Sabbath off. He praised God that she had chosen to please the Real God and follow His Ten Regulations.

They must have grown considerably in the last four years, he thought. He tried to imagine Mei-Mei. She was in her early teens when he last saw her in Shanghai's DeLanChao Prison. He could scarcely picture her as a young woman entering the People's working paradise. How did his little girls look now? When he last saw them, Lin was ten and Little Doll only six.

Maybe he idealized his children too much. He worried that the government might not provide work for Mei-Mei unless it included Saturday shifts. Holding the letters, he pleaded with his Friend to help her remain firm to her convictions and survive any hardship resulting from her decision to please Him. He wondered how the Real God would overrule the Party's efforts to sever his daughters from their "superstition."

Answering the door in the Wong apartment in Shanghai, Mei-Mei saw the telephone operator gesturing an imaginary receiver to her ear. She shouted repeatedly, "Telephone!" with a mixture of urgency and impatience.

"Coming! Coming!" Mei-Mei replied as she followed the woman down three flights of steps, through the courtyard, to the telephone booth. The operator handed the receiver to Mei-Mei.

A strange feminine voice on the other end of the line asked who she was. Mei-Mei gave her name, and the caller said in shrill staccato, "Same time." Then the phone went dead.

Mei-Mei knew the message came from the underground church. Because phones were often tapped, instructions were given in code. She handed the phone to the operator, then set out to meet the caller. According to the code, "same time" meant "in front of the post office." Looking at her watch, Mei-Mei realized she must hurry. When a bus stopped, she crowded on board, paid the ticket taker, and pressed through the crowd until she could watch from the back window. After a few stops, she saw the post office and called out, "Stop!"

As she got off the bus, she heard drums. A procession of middle-school students dressed in olive Liberation Army uniforms with red shoulder badges was marching past. Crowds gathered to watch the ceremony and, not knowing whom she was to meet, Mei-Mei joined the onlookers. The leader of the procession carried the flag of New China—bright red with a cluster of golden stars in its upper left corner. Her heart filled with pride for her country, for Mei-Mei loved China, even though it had arrested her father. Inspired by the procession, she heard the students in the parade shout patriotic slogans about the honorable peasants in Xinjiang Province and wondered why Shanghainese would be interested in people as far away as the westernmost Chinese province.

A middle-aged woman brushed against Mei-Mei, and she felt folded paper pressed into her palm—a ten-renminbi note. This was the signal that the woman was from the underground church.

"Come with me," the woman said when the procession had passed. They maneuvered through the crowd, turning onto a back street where they could make more headway.

"What's the procession all about?" Mei-Mei asked.

"Celebrating Chairman Mao's latest campaign, the Xinjiang Movement," the woman replied. "The government wants to provide work for the youth who are graduating from middle school. The Neighborhood Committees tell the graduates who are looking for work that it's patriotic for the youth to break with decadent city life, go to the countryside, and learn from the peasants." They turned up an alley, took a main street, and stopped at the entrance to Renmin Park. The woman bought two tickets and handed one to Mei-Mei, and they passed through the gate. Spotting an empty park bench, the woman said, "Let's sit and talk."

Mei-Mei had a question ready. "I'm finishing middle school this year, and I need a job. Do you think I should volunteer to go to Xinjiang?"

"I think I see someone coming who can answer that question, Mei-Mei." After looking both ways down the trail, Mei-Mei saw Pastor Chu and Elder Shu coming toward them. When the two men arrived, they sat on either side of the women. "How are you, Pastor Chu?" the middle-aged woman asked. "Mei-Mei has a question for you."

"What's that?" The pastor smiled, but his eyes dashed everywhere, searching for secret police.

"She's old enough to work now," the woman said.

"We've known each other a long time. May I talk to you as a father?"

Ever since Mr. Wong's conviction, Charlie Chu had taken a father's interest in Mr. Wong's children. He'd encouraged church members to make clothes for them and to donate money and medicine. Mei-Mei and her brother often told him of their problems. She respected her pastor's advice.

"Your future is not your own," the pastor said. "You must consider your father in the labor camp. When his prison term ends, he'll want to return home, and, while others might disagree, I think the government will allow him to. Be patient, Mei-Mei, because he needs you to keep in contact with him. In the meantime, the government will be offering you a job, so you must think carefully."

"What should I do, Pastor?" Mei-Mei asked.

"You must stay in Shanghai."

"Will the government offer me a job in Shanghai?"

"Your father is a counterrevolutionary in a hard labor camp. That puts a black mark on your record, Mei-Mei, so the Party will test your loyalty."

Mei-Mei knew he meant that the government would try to get her to join the glorious Xinjiang Movement and work with the peasants.

"It's easy to request transfers from the city to the countryside," the pastor said, "but the government is very strict on transfers to the city. Your father is in the countryside. To get permission to transfer to the city, he needs family in Shanghai. If you go to the countryside, it will be impossible for you to return to the city when your father is released, and thus it will be impossible for him to get a transfer back to Shanghai. Without your help, he will have to live the rest of his days in Tsinghai near the hard labor camp. We will do everything we can to help. Now I must go."

The pastor left immediately. Crowds entered the park. With so many eyes, it paid to be careful. The other two church members parted, going separate ways.

Mei-Mei remained on the bench, mulling over the pastor's words. While she appreciated his kindness, she knew the church members couldn't provide her with steady employment. They gave offerings and clothes, but as the government sporadically arrested one church leader after another, it would become increasingly difficult for those who were left to aid the Wong family. Besides, she didn't want to depend on them; she wanted job security with a regular salary so she could provide for her brother and sisters—and perhaps help other needy church members. The shadows grew long. Mei-Mei left the park the same way she had come.

Several days later a knock at the door caused Mei-Mei to put aside her studies. When she answered the knock, some Neighborhood Committee members, accompanied by two of her uncles, stood in the doorway. They had stern looks on their faces. Mei-Mei invited them in, dreading the news that they might bring, wondering why her uncles had accompanied the strangers. Taking them to the living room, where her sisters were studying, she disappeared, leaving her sisters to chitchat with the guests while she prepared some boiled water. Moments later she returned and poured the water into teacups.

As they sat around the table drinking, a Neighborhood Committee member said, "Maybe you've noticed the procession honoring patriotic youth." Mei-Mei remembered what the pastor had said about her father, the Xinjiang Movement, and leaving Shanghai.

The member asked, "How old are you, Mei-Mei?"

"Eighteen."

"You'll be finishing middle school soon and will need a job," the member said.

"I requested a job with no Saturday work." Mei-Mei felt tense, wishing they'd leave. "I cannot work Sabbath."

A member laughed. Her Elder Uncle asked, "Has the government offered you work yet?"

"You'll be honored to know the government's chosen you to join the Xinjiang Movement," the leader said with a smile. "We'll arrange a glorious procession for you. With your new Liberation Army clothes, you'll be the envy of Shanghai's youth."

"This is a tremendous opportunity for you, Mei-Mei," her Younger Uncle added. "New China needs the vitality of her youth, and the youth need to learn from the peasants how to strengthen our agriculture."

They talked on and on, trying to persuade Mei-Mei to go, but she couldn't get excited. She thought about her father's return. Who would take care of her brother and sisters if she went? Lee, because of his tuberculosis, seemed too weak and distracted to be head of the household. If he had another bout of illness, who would nurse him and provide for Lin and Little Doll? How she needed her father's advice! Why had two of her uncles accompanied the Neighborhood Committee representatives? When she could hold her emotions no longer, she said, "Maybe I'll think about it. This is a new idea for me."

Her guests got up to go. "Maybe this is the only job the government will offer you," Elder Uncle said as he walked down the hall. "Think seriously about taking it. Not all the middle students in Shanghai are offered jobs. You're lucky, and the pay is good." When they left, Mei-Mei hoped she would never see them again.

Returning to the living room, Mei-Mei wrote a note to Pastor Charlie Chu inviting him to her house for dinner in three days. He would understand the code, and the government would suspect nothing. They would meet on a park bench in the Shanghai Zoo at about dinnertime.

For the next three days, either her uncles or members of the Neighborhood Committee kept knocking at her door, demanding a reply to the job offer.

At the appointed time for the appointment with the pastor, Mei-Mei left her house carrying plastic bags so her neighbors would think she was going shopping. Certain that no one had noticed her, she slipped into a back alley, watching for strange people who might be in pursuit. Nearing the zoo, she joined the crowds.

Finding the usual park bench, she sat down and waited.

When she saw Pastor Chu coming, she made no sign of recognition. He sat on the other end of the bench, and for a time, neither spoke.

Charlie Chu broke the silence. "Has the government offered you a job yet, Mei-Mei?"

"The Neighborhood Committee visits me all hours of the day and night asking me to go to Xinjiang," Mei-Mei replied, without looking at Pastor Chu. "If it were only the Neighborhood Committee asking me to go, the decision would be easy, but my uncles also want me to go."

"Do you remember our discussion after the parade?"

"Yes, I must think about my father."

"Your uncles aren't Christians. They don't think your father will ever come back." The pastor turned and looked at Mei-Mei for the first time in their conversation. "Tell me, truly, do you believe your father will return to Shanghai?"

"I'm not sure."

"Mei-Mei, with God anything is possible," he said firmly. "The underground church and God will provide for you and your sisters, but you must stay in Shanghai. Act in faith." He stood up. "You are invited to eat at our house Wednesday for dinner." Without saying farewell, he left.

As the pastor lost himself in the crowd, Mei-Mei considered the code he'd given. She was to meet with the underground church members in the zoo for Wednesday-night vespers. Probably the church members would take up an offering to encourage her.

Mei-Mei dreaded to go home from school the next day because she feared the visits of the Neighborhood Committee. So she dawdled, sitting on the benches in Renmin Park and hiding in secret corners behind bushes where no one would see her. She tried to muster the courage to go home and face her uncles, but she hated the nagging. Finally, duty called. As the oldest sister, she had to prepare meals for the family. Torn between her duty to her brother and sisters and her desire to avoid conflict with the Neighborhood Committee and her uncles, the reluctant young woman left the park and trudged home.

She ascended the three-story steps, hoping to hear that the Committee members had given up waiting for her. At the top of the stairs, she opened the door and darted into the kitchen. As she boiled rice, she failed to notice someone enter.

Startled, Mei-Mei looked up to see her two uncles. Before Mei-Mei could greet them, Elder Uncle leaned his head back into the hallway and called, "Mei-Mei's come already!" Instantly, the kitchen became crowded with Neighborhood Committee members hovering around her, making it both physically and emotionally difficult for her to cook.

"Are you going to Xinjiang?" they harped. "The government needs to know your decision."

"Why can't you decide?" her uncles yelled even louder. "Either you love New China, or you don't. Are you loyal to Chairman Mao? If you are, going to Xinjiang is the perfect way to show it."

"You're the daughter of a counterrevolutionary," Younger Uncle said harshly. "The government is being kind to offer you such a heroic task."

"Besides," Elder Uncle shouted, "Chairman Mao will provide well for you. You'll get new Liberation Army uniforms and a house. By delaying your decision, you're insulting our leaders."

Mei-Mei didn't dare respond, for anything she said might later be used against her, so she just stirred the rice.

"As your Elder Uncle, I insist you commit yourself today!" the older uncle said. "Will you disgrace me by not listening to my advice?"

Mei-Mei took the rice off the stove. Carrying it down the hall, she placed it on the table in the family room. She set out enough bowls and chopsticks to include them all. Without saying a word, she and her brother and sisters sat down. Their guests pulled up their own chairs and joined them, filled their blue-and-white porcelain bowls with rice, and began eating. As they ate, they continued nagging Mei-Mei. She kept her head down, but her mind was asking for more faith that her father would return from the labor camp. She must prepare for that day as she would for Christ's return.

The evening grew dark before her guests left. "Take your time, Mei-Mei. Think about it. Going to Xinjiang is patriotic and heroic. Consider the parade the government will organize in your honor."

"What a chance! You young people have opportunities I never had," Elder Uncle chimed in loudly. "If I were young, I'd go."

"I'll be honored to see you go," said Younger Uncle.

When at last they closed the door, Mei-Mei felt relieved. Exhausted, she pulled out the drawer that held her Japanese-style bed and flopped onto it, but a knock interrupted her moment of peace.

"May I talk to you alone? I've got something very important to say." Elder Uncle spoke nervously as they walked to the family room. "I'm a no-good uncle to you, and I feel terrible."

"No, you're a good uncle," Mei-Mei replied politely. "Maybe I should listen more carefully to your advice."

"I hate what I'm doing to my family," he said as he sat at the table. "I'm here only because the Neighborhood Committee forced me. They gave me a three-month leave of absence from my job—with pay—to help them persuade you to go to Xinjiang."

Shocked and hurt by her uncle's admission of betrayal, Mei-Mei wasn't completely surprised, for she'd suspected him.

"I'll be honest with you, Mei-Mei," Elder Uncle continued as he leaned across the table. "My brother isn't like me. I'm afraid he believes in the Xinjiang Movement, but I believe we Chinese should favor family over government. You're part of my family, and I want to help you do whatever you want. Can we talk?"

Mei-Mei didn't trust him. Both uncles had betrayed her. Was Elder Uncle confessing, trying to make amends by claiming to be two-timing the government, or was he playing another trick? Had he been sent on a fact-finding mission to learn what she really thought? Fearing the worst, she said nothing.

"I don't blame you for not trusting me, Mei-Mei." He pointed to his nose. "I came alone because I didn't want my brother to know. Our meeting must remain a secret."

She decided he was telling the truth. Maybe she'd risk being frank with him. Weighing her words so as not to betray her feelings, she asked, "Elder Uncle, do you really think I should go to Xinjiang Province?"

"Not if you don't want to." He smiled.

"I'm a city girl. I don't know anything about country life. Shanghai's my home, and it's got everything I need. If I go, I'll have to leave my brother and sisters. I have no relatives or friends in Xinjiang."

"A valid concern, Mei-Mei." Elder Uncle leaned back in his chair. "What little I know about Xinjiang is that life there is very different from Shanghai. The province has many minorities who don't look, dress, think, or act like us civilized Chinese." He continued condescendingly. "They're all so poor and backward. The Uygers are Muslim fanatics, and the Kosaks are nomadic and primitive. In fact," he laughed, "there's even a big-nosed minority group of Russian descent. We Chinese don't like any of them because they aren't as sophisticated and advanced as we are. They don't share our history and heritage. I have no idea how those minorities would treat a Chinese girl or how you could live with them."

"So you think I should stay in Shanghai, Elder Uncle?"

"You do have your family to think about."

"Elder Uncle, there's another reason why I can't go." She poured boiling water from a thermos.

"What's that?"

"I believe my father is going to be released someday, and I want to be here to help him resettle in Shanghai."

"You're a loyal daughter." Elder Uncle sipped some water. "Much more loyal than I! I betrayed you because I feared the Neighborhood Committee."

"Never mind that, Elder Uncle," Mei-Mei said. "If you think I should stay in Shanghai, how can I live if the government doesn't offer me a job?"

"You can wait five years for them to assign you to another job." Elder Uncle put down his cup.

"But, Elder Uncle, how would I survive?"

He leaned back and thought a moment. "You can work for me, Mei-Mei, though I can't pay you much. Would you wash my family's clothes once a week?"

Without hesitation, Mei-Mei replied, "I'll be glad to."

"Then it's settled," Elder Uncle said with a smile. "I'll pay you five renminbi a week, but we'll have to do everything secretly."

"When do you want me to wash clothes for you?"

"That's a problem." Elder Uncle laughed nervously. "I'm still working for your Neighborhood Committee until the end of the summer. I'm afraid of them, so I'll continue to yell and shout at you whenever they're present. I've got no other choice. I don't want trouble. With money comes obligation, but I've got a plan. It'll satisfy both them and you. Listen carefully."

Mei-Mei listened. When he'd explained, she agreed to cooperate.

The next day, when Mei-Mei returned home from school, her

uncles and the Neighborhood Committee members were waiting with the usual nagging and demands. When she said nothing, they became more agitated. Elder Uncle shouted even louder than he had before.

Amused inwardly, Mei-Mei dared not show it. Busying herself in the kitchen boiling water, she hoped her face gave no hint of her thoughts. When the water had boiled, she served her unwanted guests.

After what seemed like eons, the Neighborhood Committee members finally left. A few moments later, Elder Uncle was back at the door.

"Come quickly," he said. At the bottom of the steps waited a rickshaw. They climbed inside and closed the curtain. She felt the driver lift the bars and pull. They bumped and swayed as the driver ran toward his destination. Eventually, after numerous jolts and turns, they felt the front end lowered. Elder Uncle opened the curtain, helped her step down, and paid the driver. After climbing several flights of stairs, he led her into a long hallway lined with windows. At the end of the hall sat a basin full of clothes, a faucet, a wooden board, and a large bar of soap. Long rays of sunlight shone in at an angle, revealing dust particles dancing in the air. "It's all set up. You can hang the clothes out the windows."

Mei-Mei saw bamboo poles attached below the windows pointing over the street below. Across the street were clothes hanging from similar poles. Elder Uncle left.

Squatting, she went right to work. She dumped the clothes from the basin onto the cement floor and filled the basin with water. Then she dunked the clothes in the cold water, wrung them out, and laid them on a board. She rubbed soap into them, soaked them again, beat them against the board, and wrung them out again. "Elder Uncle must have collected all the clothes from all the relatives!" she said to herself. "I've never seen such a pile!"

She finished washing as darkness crept into the room. Her uncle was pleased and handed her the promised five renminbi. Holding it in her hand, she knew that even though the money wasn't much, she had the security she needed.

By the end of the summer, as her uncle had predicted, the Neighborhood Committee quit visiting her home. Elder Uncle resumed his regular work, and nothing more was said about the Xinjiang Movement.

As the weeks turned to months and the months into years, Mei-Mei's hands suffered from wringing out clothes in the chilly water. But when she was tempted to complain, she remembered her father, and, with renewed vigor, worked a little harder, grateful for her uncle's kindness and God's goodness. With each twist of the cloth and trickle of water, she thanked God in faith that she'd see her father again, a reunion made possible by a weak, frightened, betraying uncle who felt guilty enough to come up with a solution.

Chapter 23

ICY CANALS AND WILD DOGS

Mr. Wong's work unit had the difficult task of breaking the ice to clear irrigation ditches so the water could flow to barley fields for the benefit of the camp guards. Hacking away at the ice with pick and shovel in the cold late spring seemed harder when Mr. Wong knew he'd never eat a morsel of the grain.

After he broke the ice into blocks and lifted the blocks onto the bank, he had to be careful not to allow the icy water to seep into his boots, where it could freeze. He recalled one prisoner who'd allowed his hands to get frostbitten. When the team returned to the burrow, he'd poured hot water over his hands, and his fingers fell off. No one in the camp could ever forget his screams.

Each prisoner was supposed to clear one thousand feet of clogged canal every day, and anyone who didn't achieve his quota would be punished. Then they had to load some of the ice chunks onto a wagon and haul them to the camp for the cooks.

At the end of one particular day, Mr. Wong felt tired, but more lonely than tired. The day had been so busy, and he'd been around the other prisoners from early morning till late afternoon. He wished he could have time to himself just to think. After the ice was loaded on the wagon, the driver ordered the prisoners to sit on the back. A guard hitched the horses to the cart. The lash from the driver's whip startled the horses, and they lurched forward. The prisoners sitting on the back of the wagon tried to avoid contact with the ice.

The long, bumpy ride to the prison compound caused painful

jostling for Mr. Wong. He needed to stretch his legs. "Stop! Stop!" he called repeatedly until he caught the driver's attention.

"What do you want?" the driver asked as he pulled the reins to slow the horses.

"The road is so rough that it makes me sore," Mr. Wong said, flashing his most charming smile. "Request permission to walk back to camp."

The driver stopped and said, "You can walk back. I doubt you'll try to escape. But hurry. If you get lost and try to sleep out here, you'll never survive the cold. It's dangerous in these hills after dark, for tigers and bands of wild dogs prowl this area."

"Thank you. I'm not afraid. My Friend Jesus will protect me."

The driver didn't respect Mr. Wong's beliefs, but he liked his work habits and trusted him. The guards and team leaders who'd observed Mr. Wong long enough became fond of him. Mr. Wong felt grateful to the driver as they exchanged farewell glances. "Be careful," the driver warned as the cart rolled on down the road. Mr. Wong watched it rattle and bounce until it disappeared around a bend.

All alone, Mr. Wong felt the peaceful stillness of the fields flanked by the majestic mountains of Tibet. He loved a brisk walk and reveled in the natural beauty. He felt grateful for this rare opportunity to appreciate the handiwork of the Real God. Relaxed, he felt he had the whole world to himself.

After walking several miles, he noticed a rapid movement ahead. A band of wild dogs, having caught his scent, charged up the road toward him with fierce eyes, rumbling growls, and barred teeth. He remembered hearing rumors that the hungry wild dogs near the compound were man-eaters, and he didn't wish to be lunch for these beasts.

On and on they came. It almost seemed as though he could hear their stomachs growling in anticipation! He imagined them leaping through the air, knocking him down, tearing him into shreds, gnawing on his bones, and licking their chops afterward. Shivers shot through him. He couldn't move, fearing his approaching death.

With no place to hide and no way to outrun the hungry animals, he fell to his knees before the wild dogs, spread his arms wide in the form of a crucifix, closed his eyes, and prayed, "My Friend Jesus, save my life from these dangerous dogs! Take away their appetite. You closed the mouths of hungry lions, preventing them from injuring Your servant Daniel. Since You protected Daniel in a den of lions, I know You can also shut the mouths of these wild dogs for me! Thank You, Jesus, my Friend, for helping me. Amen."

Mr. Wong heard a slight whimper and opened his eyes. The wild dogs surrounded him with their tails tucked between their legs. They were transformed from ferocious beasts into what seemed like friendly pets. When he stood up, the dogs wagged their tails, inviting him to stroke them behind their ears.

A broad smile crossed Mr. Wong's face as they stretched out their forepaws and yawned in a little welcome dance. They even seemed to recognize him, or, he suspected, they saw in him Someone else. Squatting, he reached out his hand, and the wild dogs spilled over each other in their attempts to lick his palm. Their tongues felt wet and rough.

Suddenly, the dogs turned and ran up a hill. Mr. Wong resumed his walk, praising his Friend Jesus!

Chapter 24

LEE'S LAST REQUESTS

Whenever a new load of prisoners was trucked into the labor camp, Mr. Wong scanned their faces, worried that his son Lee might be one of the new guests. He knew from his children's letters that his son was remaining a strong Christian, yet on lonely nights, he longed to be reunited with him. He feared, as only a father can, that Lee could not withstand the suffering his father had endured for his faith.

In 1963, as the fifty-six-year-old father finished another prayer that his son wouldn't join him, he seemed to hear a clear voice in his mind bringing a message of relief. "Your son won't come to the hard labor camp!"

In Shanghai, Lee worked in a dismal factory folding paper and slapping glue on it to form boxes. Bored with the monotony, he felt ashamed at work because he'd been placed in a group with elderly women. The repetitious job provided no mental stimulation. As he stacked the paper boxes, he felt deep concern for how he could provide for his sisters with his low salary.

After his father's incarceration, Lee had become the head of the household. The children had no income, so Lee, eighteen and old enough to enter the People's working paradise, applied for work that allowed free weekends. Because he wanted his Sabbaths off and because he was the son of a convicted counter-revolutionary, the government offered him only a job for old ladies, making boxes.

As he worked, he devised a plan that would help his sisters

become self-sufficient, but it required money. After lunch, he walked to the post office for the day's mail. The clerk handed him a simple envelope. Opening the letter, he found that it contained eighteen renminbi—the government's monthly subsidy for poor families. Under the policy, one needy person received seven renminbi a month, two received eleven renminbi, three received fifteen renminbi, and the four in Lee's family received eighteen renminbi.

At home that night, Lee took a portion of the money and hid it in his room, then gave the rest to Lin so she could shop for the family's needs. Tired and tense from the day's work, he got out his violin and played soothing music.

From her bedroom, Lin heard her brother's melodies and wondered why he spent so much time locked in his room playing his violin. True, he needed relaxation, but he threw so much emotion and energy into his playing that it seemed to sap his strength rather than revitalize it. Lin considered his violin playing an obsession that distanced him from his sisters. His hobby seemed to be an escape from the responsibility and frustration of being head of the household.

Even with the combination of the government's subsidy, Lee's wages, and Mei-Mei's income from washing clothes, there was not enough money to cover the rent and food. Lee's early growth spurt made him tall, thin, gangly, pale, and sickly. Too poor to buy the variety of food necessary to fill her brother's bottomless stomach, Lin feared he wasn't obtaining adequate nutrition to prevent a tubercular relapse. If he were hospitalized, it would greatly set back the family financially. Thankful that she didn't hear him coughing, she felt content. However, as the cold winds brought the winter of 1963, Lin heard her brother punctuating his violin strokes with subdued coughs.

Late at night on February 21, 1963, Lee coughed heavily. Mei-Mei, who had cared for her mother, recognized the sound, got up, entered her brother's room across the hall, and stood by his bedside. "Let me see your hands," she said.

As Lee held out his hands, Mei-Mei saw the telltale blood streaks on them. Suddenly, Lee erupted into spasms of coughing, vomiting large quantities of dried blood like coffee grounds.

Dashing out into the snowy night, Mei-Mei skidded on the ice as she searched for someone to rush her brother to the hospital. Securing a bicycle rickshaw driver, she bounded back up to Lee's room. Coughing and gasping, her brother seemed dying from the loss of blood. She helped him down the steps and into the rickshaw seat. Squeezing in beside him, she yelled to the driver, "Take us to the nearest hospital. And hurry up!"

The cold night air caused the phlegm to flow from Lee's lungs, but when they reached the hospital, he stopped coughing. Mei-Mei felt relieved, hoping it meant improvement. But the doctor looked unhappy. "As long as he's coughing," he said, "your brother is clearing out his lungs, but now the blood is trapped. It's moved deeper in his chest, and he can't vomit it out. He must remain in the hospital and be carefully monitored."

The doctor and a nurse helped Lee into a ward occupied by another tubercular patient. Mei-Mei followed. When the doctor stepped outside, she joined him. "How is his condition, Doctor?"

"Very serious," the doctor said. "The patient may die. For him to survive, he'll need someone to be with him constantly. Unfortunately, we don't have enough nurses to provide that kind of care."

Her brother would probably never work again, which meant no more income from him. If she stayed with him, she couldn't wash clothes. How could they survive? Her sisters had to attend classes. Besides, none of them had experience caring for a tubercular patient. "I can take care of him," she volunteered.

"That's very loving of you," the doctor replied. "I hope you realize the dangers. Young people are especially susceptible to this highly contagious disease. The germs are airborne carriers and can be inhaled easily. You'll have to wear a mask."

Mei-Mei agreed. The only thing that mattered was to stay by her brother's side, hoping she might save his life. With the mask on, the room seemed stuffy and hot. She wanted to remove it but kept her promise.

A nurse wearing a mask wheeled in an ancient respirator and hooked it up to Lee's nose and mouth. "If this machine stops working for any reason, give us a call," she said, showing Mei-Mei a button next to the bed. Then she left. Another masked nurse set up a cot for Mei-Mei. Only family members could visit Lee, but occasionally Pastor Charlie Chu arrived unannounced to bring cheer and share news.

After Lee had been in the hospital several days, his room-mate died of tuberculosis and was wheeled away. An endless week later, Lin walked through the door wearing a mask. "I came to see Lee," she announced with muffled words.

"How are you, Lin?" Mei-Mei welcomed her sister.

"You look tired," Lin replied. "I'll stay tonight. Go home and get some rest. How is Lee doing?"

"Maybe he'll die tonight," Mei-Mei whispered, hoping Lee wouldn't hear. She gathered her things and showed her fifteen-year-old sister what to do.

A tear rolled down Lin's cheek as she looked at the shriveled skeleton of her dear brother, who should have been in the prime of youth. She couldn't ask him if he was dying, but she'd heard that dying was uncomfortable. "Lee, do you feel comfortable?" she asked.

"I have peace in my heart," he replied softly. His breathing, syncopated with coughs, made talking difficult. "My under . . . wear, coat, and trousers are still new. Don't let them be cre-mated . . . with my body. After I . . . die, take them off and . . . mail them . . . to our father. When I'm . . . dead, don't tell our fa . . . ther. He has . . . too much to . . . worry about."

"But you're so young," Lin exclaimed.

Lee's coughing spell grew worse. After a moment, he man-aged to say, "A person . . . will die . . . even if he lives a . . . hundred years."

The words were too much for Lin, and she wailed loudly.

"Don't . . . cry," he wheezed between rasping gasps and coughs. "Don't feel . . . sorry for me. If I . . . die, promise me . . . you won't . . . cry loudly. If you do . . . it'll . . . upset the others."

Lin dried her tears. "I promise to be strong."

"Promise . . . me something . . . else." Lee's eyes seemed to penetrate Lin's soul.

"What's that?"

"You must . . . keep . . . Sabbath."

After her father's arrest and Lee's stay in the hospital, Lin had attended school and done her homework on Saturdays. She hadn't known that her brother knew. To honor his dying wish, she decided to keep the Sabbath, no matter what the cost. She trusted God to honor her decision and grant her wisdom to keep up her studies, even though she missed one day of school a week. She'd earned very high marks on her entrance exam and had been allowed, despite her status as the stinking daughter of a counterrevolutionary, to enter the best middle school in Shanghai. Face to face with death, honoring God seemed far more important than studying on Sabbath. Looking down at Lee, she said, "I promise to keep Sabbath as long as I live."

Lee seemed content.

When her sister returned the next morning to resume her vigil, Lin told her of Lee's request about his clothes, omitting the part about Sabbath keeping.

"It may be our brother's last request, so we'll gladly honor it," Mei-Mei said. "Besides, our father needs new clothes."

Lin waved as she left the room. "I'll come back next week. Bye-bye!" she said as she left for school.

On Sabbath a week later, Mei-Mei bathed Lee's brow with a cloth, wiping up his sweat. His twenty-three-year-old frame had wasted rapidly so that his clothes, once a perfect fit, looked too large. The intervals between Lee's coughing spells had markedly increased. The new silence sounded an alarm. Coughing denoted life; silence did not.

Lee opened his mouth and struggled to form words between breaths. Mei-Mei leaned closer.

"Please—" Lee sighed.

"What?"

"Surprise—" he gasped. "Ninety renminbi."

"What's the surprise for?"

"Sewing-machine business."

"You want me to spend the money on a sewing machine so I can support the family?"

Lee smiled.

Mei-Mei hadn't realized that he'd had a plan for the family. How had he saved so much money? The amount was only ten renminbi short of the cost of a sewing machine. Trying to contain her excitement, she asked, "Where's the money?"

"Home." He struggled to take a breath. "Find."

"Is it hidden in your room?"

Lee nodded his head weakly. "Please—" Lee gasped.

Mei-Mei sensed he was changing the subject. "What?"

"Wrap my clothes." Lee's body exploded into a coughing spell, but he managed to say, "Mail."

Remembering what Lin had told her before she left, Mei-Mei guessed, "Mail your clothes to Father?"

Lee seemed content, then forced out the words, "Don't tell."

"You don't want Father to know." Mei-Mei saw the pleased look on his face. "Why?" she asked.

"Praying."

"You're praying?"

As Lee motioned weakly, Mei-Mei helped him talk.

"No—Papa's praying for you to get well? Yes? No! He's praying to see you on earth? No? In heaven? I understand. Father's praying to see you again in heaven, if not on earth."

Lee smiled, then fought to say, "Shield."

"Shield. From Satan? No? Shield—Father." Mei-Mei at last understood. "You want me to shelter Father from the bad news. But how?"

"Gift. Duty. Support." Lee whispered the words.

"You want me to tell Father your underwear, coat, and trousers are a gift from you to show you're doing your duty to support him." Seeing Lee agreed, she exclaimed, "You have a lovely idea, Lee!"

"Don't tell." Lee gasped deeply, then set off on another round of coughs, terminating the conversation. Mei-Mei grabbed a cloth and placed it over his mouth. Between coughs, Lee forced out the word, "Promise!"

Mei-Mei leaned closer. "I promise."

With a sudden outburst of strength, Lee insisted, "Take—clothes off my back—send—Father." Lee paused to inhale. "Last thing—I—do—for him." His sides heaved from the effort. "Please—honor—wish."

Mei-Mei fought back tears.

Just then, the door opened, and Pastor Charlie Chu entered.

After greeting him, Mei-Mei explained Lee's request. "I'll be glad to help," the pastor said with a smile. "He doesn't want his father to know? I'll keep the secret."

"How did you get in here, Pastor Chu?" Mei-Mei changed the subject. "Aren't the hospital staff very strict?"

Looking around the room nervously, the pastor said, "I'll tell you later."

"I'm glad you're here." Mei-Mei spoke softly. "You came at the right time." Watching her brother struggle, she knew she could no longer take his breathing for granted.

"What can I do?" Pastor Chu asked.

"I don't know," Mei-Mei said. "Things with Lee aren't working out as I had hoped."

"You want Lee to get better. That's natural, Mei-Mei."

"I've accepted whatever God decides for my brother," Mei-Mei said. "But it's still not easy! I don't want my brother to suffer. I want him to be happy and live." Mei-Mei looked at her pastor. "Why does God allow him to suffer so? Doesn't He care?"

"God cares, Mei-Mei. It hurts God to see suffering. He even sees the chickens in the open marketplace and winces as the merchant plucks each feather from the squawking bird. God is pained when its neck is finally twisted. If God cares for a chicken, He surely cares about your brother's pain and your sorrow." The pastor flashed a smile. "Jesus healed the sick and the lame when He was on earth. God wants to end all suffering. Right now, we are like pawns in the devil's battle against God. When the war between Christ and Satan is over, God will wipe away all our tears. Even now, if God willed, He could make Lee well."

"Will you pray for him, Pastor?"

"Certainly." He bowed his head and committed Lee to God's mercy and grace.

A few hours later, Lee looked up and smiled. "Goodbye, Mei-Mei!" he struggled to say and repeated, "Goodbye, Mei-Mei!" His rasps faded into a death rattle. Then all was still. Pastor Chu pressed his finger against Lee's pulse, but he felt no beat.

"We've a promise to keep. Let's take his clothes off now," the pastor said.

On March 21, 1963, one week after Lin had spent the night with Lee and one month after his hospitalization, as Lin headed to the hospital to relieve her sister, she met Mei-Mei walking home carrying a parcel. "What's in the package, Mei-Mei?"

"Lee's clothes," Mei-Mei replied. "He died on Sabbath. Lee said, 'Goodbye, Mei-Mei,' two times."

The girls stood silently grieving; then Mei-Mei asked, "Do you want to come with me to the post office on Monday? We need to mail this parcel to our father."

"I'll help," Lin answered. "We have promises to keep."

Some time later, Mei-Mei climbed the steps to the family's home with an envelope in her hand. Unable to contain her excitement, she blurted out, "Look! We got a letter from the labor camp!"

"From Father?" Lin asked.

"Yes!" Mei-Mei exclaimed as she tore open the envelope. "I wonder if he got our package."

"I wish Mother and Lee could hear the letter. If Father got the clothes, Lee would be so pleased." Lin spoke sadly.

"We all miss Lee and MaMa too."

"Read it!" Little Doll begged. "What does he say?"

Mei-Mei began to read. "He thanks us for Lee's clothes."

"So he got them." Little Doll clapped her hands.

"That's a miracle!" Lin exclaimed. "I thought the guards might keep the clothes for themselves."

"Does he know Lee's dead?"

"Little Doll, it's not polite to talk like that," Lin chided. "Tell us what Father says about Lee, Mei-Mei. Were we able to shelter him from the bad news?"

Mei-Mei read aloud, " 'I'm certain that Lee does not have enough clothes to spare, so now I understand that I'm not going to see my son again in this world.' " Mei-Mei paused to blink back a tear.

"So he knows," Lin interrupted.

"How did he find out?" Little Doll looked at Mei-Mei. "Was it something we said?"

"He knows we're too poor to buy new clothes, Little Doll," Lin explained. "He knows that Lee had only one outfit."

Mei-Mei went on reading. " 'I prayed every night that God would help Lee to be faithful. God is good. He knows what's best for us, my daughters. He must have known that it was better for Lee to suffer from illness than to be tortured for his faith. I'm happy for him. God has spared him the troublesome times to come. I believe God took Lee when he was safe to save.' "

Mei-Mei continued reading, " 'Now, my daughters, be strong! Conditions will get worse. Someday you may be tried and tested like me, because you believe in God. Dear daughters, prepare now for that terrible future. Jesus won't ask you to suffer anything beyond what you can bear. When everyone else seems to have forsaken you, don't forget that my Friend Jesus is your Friend too. Our God is real. He'll be with you always.' "

Mei-Mei's voice choked, and she blinked back the tears as she read the last words: "Love, Father."

Chapter 25

SINGING TO HIS EXECUTION

Unlike the other prisoners on his work team, Mr. Wong worked hard at the exhausting job of cutting trees in the woods. He felled the trees with axes, cut the trunks into firewood, and loaded them onto wooden carts, which guards drove to the prison compound. At midday a guard called, "*Xuxi!* Time to stop!"

Everyone laid down his tools. As the prison was an hour's walk away, the inmates remained in the woods. They leaned against trees, ate their lunches, and snoozed. Mr. Wong opened his medical book and read verses from a page in Scripture. Presently he heard a greeting, "Have you eaten rice yet?" Looking up, he saw a prisoner's face close to his.

"I'm very full already," Mr. Wong said with a smile and returned to his reading.

"Old Wong, what can you tell me about religion?" the inmate whispered into his ear. A quick glance at the guards assured Mr. Wong they were busy eating their food. Taking out two pieces of toilet paper, he wrote a verse on each. "Jesus said, I am the Way, the Truth, and the Life. No one can reach heaven except through Me," and "Thou shalt have no other gods before Me." Folding each piece of paper separately into tiny squares, he handed them to the inmate. "Memorize these verses. Destroy the toilet paper. Come to me, quote the words, and I'll give you another verse."

The break ended and the prisoners felled more trees, until the guard yelled, "Line up!"

Obeying, they marched ahead of the guards toward the prison

compound. Mr. Wong wondered whether he'd helped a friend or a judas at noon. Sooner or later he would learn the truth.

That night two guards rushed into Mr. Wong's niche, accompanied by the inmate he'd befriended in the woods. The inmate hung his head in feigned repentance. The guards were new transfers, unfamiliar with Mr. Wong.

"Criminal Wong," a guard bellowed. "Did you teach him?"

"Teach him what?" Mr. Wong asked.

"Show Criminal Wong!" The prisoner produced crumpled pieces of toilet paper with Chinese characters on them. "Did you write this?"

Mr. Wong recognized the texts he'd written and given the prisoner. His heart sank, yet he pitied the poor wretch.

"Read!"

Unfolding one of the pieces of toilet paper, Mr. Wong read, "Jesus said, 'I am the Way, the Truth, and the Life. No one can reach heaven except through Me.' "

"Let me see that." The other guard grabbed the paper, read it, and sneered. "No one believes this old man's crazy ideas. If he wants to write that nonsense to the prisoners, he can. It's his own business. Besides, there's no harm in that message."

"Read the other one!"

Taking the other piece of toilet paper, Mr. Wong read, "Thou shalt have no other gods before Me."

"That's anti-revolutionary! You're opposing the laws of New China by teaching your own rules!" the guards shouted. "Criminal Wong, confess! Confess! Why did you give this to him?"

"I wanted him to know about the Ten Regulations of Jesus, my Friend," Mr. Wong admitted calmly. "The Real God speaks to us through the Old and New Testaments."

"Do you know why you're in prison?"

"Because I'm a Christian."

"Because you stubbornly persist in breaking New China's laws and teaching laws counter to our government's laws. You caused great confusion for this poor prisoner because you broke prison rules."

"I love China, but I cannot sin against the Real God's laws."

"Do you think you're an exception and can break the rules?"

"I must obey God!" The rookie guards looked eager to reeducate him.

"Are you going to follow prison rules?"

"Only if they're in accord with God's Regulations." Mr. Wong gave his routine answer.

"Our Great Helmsman, Chairman Mao, has marked 1966 as the year to set off the Cultural Revolution," the guards announced. "You've written many confessions before, Criminal Wong, and put off your regret. This will be your very last chance."

Mr. Wong had heard about his "last chance" many times, but the Cultural Revolution was news. As the guards ranted on, he wondered what they meant by the Cultural Revolution.

"Give up your God! Repent, or perish at the execution ground! I order you to rethink your position and repent—be born again!"

"I'll gladly write another confession," Mr. Wong said, "but I cannot change my position."

"Will you comply with China's laws?"

Mr. Wong had lost count of how many times he'd heard those words from the guards.

"I cannot."

"We have a law!"

"I know your law." He thought, *If China followed its own laws, I'd be in Shanghai, not this labor camp.*

"You must obey it!"

"I'm a Christian."

"Do you know what we'll do to you if you don't obey?"

Weary with the same questions and demands and the many terrible tortures against him, he answered in sheer frustration, "You can't kill me!"

Mr. Wong couldn't believe he'd said such a bold, rash statement, but he rejoiced that he'd expressed the faith of Shadrach, Meshach, and Abednego. Regaining his composure, he explained, "My Friend Jesus can walk among flames to protect me if He chooses—and I'll come out of the fire without so much as a hair of my head singed!"

The guards' eyes darkened, then brightened at Mr. Wong's challenge. "Tomorrow we'll show you what happens to those who break prison rules!"

Almost as suddenly as they'd arrived, the guards left.

Before going to sleep, Mr. Wong adjusted the hay he'd put over the dirt floor. Sticking his hand into his blanket, he felt for another page of the Old and New Testaments, when a roommate surprised him. "What are you doing?" he asked.

Fearful that the man might discover his secret hiding place, Mr. Wong stammered, "Na-Nothing. I was adjusting my blanket. The thickness is uneven." His answer seemed satisfactory, for the inmate turned away, and dozed off. Relieved that his secret was still safe, Mr. Wong tucked a new page into his medical book. After replacing the old one in the blanket, he pulled the blanket over himself and blew out his candle.

Early the next morning the guards awakened Mr. Wong, shouting, "You were caught breaking prison rules. Now you must learn the results of your sins!" They tied his hands behind his back and hustled him out of the cave. To the guards' apparent surprise, he showed no signs of fear but smiled and stood tall.

"Smiley!" the bewildered guard exclaimed, "wipe that smile off your face! Fourteen prisoners have been sentenced for breaking the rules. You're joining them because of your stubborn insolence."

Mr. Wong guessed that they were marching him to his death. Looking heavenward, he exclaimed, "My Friend Jesus, be merciful to me, a sinner!"

"Smiley, don't expect your God to help you!"

Mr. Wong began singing a hymn: "Anywhere with Jesus I can safely go!"

"Stop singing!"

Mr. Wong sang on, "Anywhere He leads me in this world below; Anywhere without Him dearest joys would fade; Anywhere with Jesus I am not afraid."

The guards stifled his voice, so he hummed. Soon the guards grew tired and gave up.

"Jesus, You sacrificed Your life for me that I might live!" Mr. Wong shouted joyfully as he marched along. "Compared to Your sacrifice, my trouble here is just a little fuss. Thank You for the opportunity to suffer like Peter, crucified upside down, or Paul, beheaded. I accept Your will for me, even if it is a bullet to the head. Yet I know You can save me like Daniel or let me be stoned to death like Stephen."

"We'll see what you think, Criminal Wong, after what happens today."

The guards pushed Mr. Wong ahead of them toward the fourteen prisoners sentenced for punishment. His radiant face contrasted with their terrified looks.

Forcing the doomed prisoners to kneel, the guards tied their arms to their feet, pushed their heads down, and shouted, "Did you think you could break the prison rules without punishment for your sins?"

Mr. Wong joined the line. The minutes seemed like hours. The prisoners dared not move, and the guards awaited orders.

The head guard spoke. "Each of you has resisted reeducation. Even though your sins make you worthless to the system, your government will be kind." He took out a pack of cigarettes. "If you want to smoke, ask."

Upon request, the guards poked cigarettes into the prisoners' mouths, lighted them, and let the inmates drag on them until the hot ashes almost burned their lips. The prisoners spat out the butts and let them smolder on the ground.

While they smoked, Mr. Wong smiled calmly. The guard who had called him Smiley tied his arms behind his back. Mr. Wong praised God for the opportunity to be martyred for his Friend, asking that he be reunited with his family after the resurrection.

His words were punctuated by a bullet blast, followed by the thump of a body crumpling to the ground. Fourteen gunshots interrupted his prayer. Then he felt the hot barrel of a gun pressed into the back of his own head.

"It's no use praying for your family, Criminal Wong. You'll never see them again!" the head guard yelled.

Mr. Wong prayed more fervently.

"Why talk to your fake God? Why not talk to your real government? What good has your God done for you?" The guard paused, and Mr. Wong continued praying.

"Your worthless ideas and your stubbornness caused your wife's death! If you'd cooperated with your kind government,

Criminal Wong, you would have had enough money to pay for her medicine. We repeatedly labored with you to end your bourgeois liberalism before your arrest, but your anti-party ideas got you here today. Your wife died two months before your arrest. You'll never see her again!"

"I will see my wife again when my Friend, the Real God, returns to take us home to heaven." Mr. Wong felt the hot, deadly metal thrust roughly against his head. "She accepted Jesus as her Saviour and Friend before she died."

"Religion, the opiate of the people, gives you false hope! The truth is, Criminal Wong, even if your kind government lets you live, you'll never see her again!"

"You don't know about the resurrection. My Friend Jesus has keys that will open up my tomb. To me, dying is not a problem—staying dead is!" He again prayed for a reunion with his children.

"I see you have new clothes, Criminal Wong! Your son sent them, didn't he?"

"Yes."

"Why did he send them, Criminal Wong?"

"Because he's a good son." Mr. Wong chose to say no more. The rope felt tight against his wrist. His knees ached, and his neck hurt. "Lee wanted to send a gift to his father."

"Your son is dead!" the guard yelled, revealing that he had read Mr. Wong's mail. "He died because of your stubbornness! You'll never see him again either. Was it worth it? Haven't you paid a high-enough price for your counterrevolutionary activities?"

"I haven't paid as high a price as my Friend Jesus, who gave His life to ransom me from this terrible world. My son died because the Real God thought he couldn't stand the test of faithfulness in this prison camp."

"You always give credit for everything to your so-called Real God."

To calm himself, Mr. Wong sang the refrain from the hymn "There Is a Fountain," then offered praise to God. "Jesus, take me if it's Your will! Forgive this man, for he doesn't know about You. Let my death lift You up before human beings."

"Don't ask your God to forgive me," the guard shouted. "Ask your government to have mercy on you!" He kicked Mr. Wong, rolling him onto his side on the ground.

"Get up, Criminal Wong!"

Mr. Wong lay in a heap, his hands tied to his feet.

"Ask your God to help you up!" the guard yelled. "See if he can save you."

Nothing happened.

The guard laughed. "You write your daughters reminding them to thank your so-called Real God for their food. God doesn't give them their food. The Communist party does. Teach them to thank the Party! Why don't you give credit where credit is due?"

Mr. Wong lifted his head. "The Party would have no power if my Friend Jesus hadn't given them the authority."

"Only the Party can save this world, not your so-called Real God!" The guard commanded, "Stand up!"

Mr. Wong tried, but the ropes restricted him. He fell back.

"Where is your Real God?" the guard taunted. "Why hasn't he helped you? Is he asleep?" Laughing, he grabbed the rope and lifted Mr. Wong to his knees. "Don't ever forget this day, Criminal Wong. Notice who lifted you up—the Party, not your so-called Real God!"

Mr. Wong heard the guard slip his gun into its holster. Then he yelled, "Wake up, Criminal Wong! Your fake friend Jesus can't help you because he isn't real! The Party exists!" Fumbling with the ropes, the guard untied Mr. Wong. "Don't go thanking your God for your miserable life. He did nothing to save you. The Party mercifully decided to grant you a second chance. Thank the Party!"

"The government is kind to reeducate me," Mr. Wong said, without compromising his convictions.

Lifting Mr. Wong to his feet, the guard said, "Now you're talking, Criminal Wong. Don't think I wouldn't shoot you in a minute. I didn't kill you today because I can't waste the Party's valuable ammunition. Your daughters can't afford to pay for the bullet!" Mr. Wong knew the Communist party would have sent a bill for the bullet to his daughters. Placing his arm around Mr. Wong, the guard added, "Besides, Criminal Wong, how can I reeducate you if you're dead? Right now, you're worth more to me alive. I've got a new job for you." He pointed to the corpses lying nearby. "Bury the dead!"

Rejoicing, he dragged the cadavers to the dead pile. Mr. Wong later left the prison compound and walked for over an hour to the hillside, where he joined the work unit assigned to burying the dead. He knew that for at least a week he would not lack for work, because during the winter the ground had been too hard to dig, and the dead had piled up. When he arrived, he noticed a tall, hefty prisoner from a camp twenty miles away carrying a bamboo pole on his shoulder from which dangled two scrawny bodies weighing less than 50 kilos apiece. Mr. Wong guessed that he had carried the corpses for over two hours.

Joining the others, Mr. Wong began digging ditches two meters deep, using pick and shovel. Dragging a corpse from the pile, he tossed it into a ditch. One by one, he pulled three to five more bodies to each ditch and dropped them in. Shoveling dirt back into the ditches, he covered them in a nameless oblivion.

Some of the prisoners complained to the team leader that the dead deserved more respect. "They suffered terribly during their life in hard labor camp. They deserve to rest more comfortably under the ground." Specifically, they demanded that the prisoners be buried "one body to a ditch."

To Mr. Wong's surprise, the team leader granted the request—the first concession the authorities had made to the prisoners, and, he feared, probably the last.

Gradually, Mr. Wong grew accustomed to his gruesome job of tossing the malnourished bodies of dead hunger victims into ditches. One day he discovered that part of a cadaver's buttocks had been cut away. Had it been by torture, or was this an act of cannibalism?

The winter wind chilled the team and froze the surface of the ground, making digging arduous. The guard left the inmates to warm himself at a fire. Knowing they were alone, the prisoners relaxed, picking at the earth only casually. Shocked, Mr. Wong saw one grow bold, hack off part of a buttock, and devour it.

Chapter 26

RED GUARD RAID

After June 1966 in Shanghai, Mr. Wong's daughters heard the notorious Red Guards marching every day with beating drums and bashing brass gongs, seeking out one counterrevolutionary target after another. The Cultural Revolution was composed of schoolchildren clad in blue Sun Yat-sen jackets and red armbands parading the streets to clear China of the enemies of Chairman Mao.

The Red Guards' targets were former capitalists and landlords, "counterrevolutionaries," criminals, and intellectuals— especially the middle-school teachers of the Red Guards, with their families. Professing great love for Chairman Mao, the Red Guards performed their deeds of terror for weeks with scarcely a wink of sleep. They reveled in the power they felt from repeating the sayings in the Little Red Book of the Great Helmsman. Some hoped by their terrorism to clear black marks from their own names, because they had been born to parents who fell under the "stinking categories" Chairman Mao opposed.

In October 1966, the Cultural Revolution reached a frenzied peak. All Chinese who weren't Red Guards feared the night even more than the day. Mei-Mei sat with her sisters in the living room sewing for her customers. She'd seen red banners posted on the streets by the Red Guards. Stopping to read them, she noticed that they listed counterrevolutionary criminals sentenced to hard labor camps. She saw her father's name painted in bold black characters across one of the banners. This republishing of his status eight years after his conviction filled Mei-Mei with dread, for now the Red Guards could terrorize his family. Quickly, she hurried home, hoping no one would recognize her. But when she arrived, she told her sisters none of what she'd seen.

That night the girls heard the drums, gongs, and shouts of the Red Guards entering the former Japanese compound. "Perhaps they'll search our house tonight," Mei-Mei said.

She heard the Red Guard shout, "Let's go to Little Doll's home!"

Like an army of feet stomping up the three flights of stairs, the Red Guards beat their drums and gongs, denouncing the three girls by name. Quickly, Mei-Mei hid her sewing machine in the top dresser drawer and stuffed cloth in the bottom drawer. If the Red Guard suspected her sewing business, she'd be branded a filthy capitalist. The girls huddled together on a bed as twenty Red Guards rushed down the hallway and swarmed into all the rooms.

The leader, hardly sixteen, proudly carried a copy of Chairman Mao's Little Red Books in his hand. Though still attending middle school, the red armband gave him all the authority he needed. Examining the room, he demanded, "Where's your portrait and bust of Chairman Mao?" He held up his Little Red Book. "Where's your copy of Mao's sayings?" The other Red Guards thrust their Little Red Books into the air and shouted, "Read the Little Red Books! Memorize the wit and wisdom of the Great Helmsman. Long live Chairman Mao!" Handing Mei-Mei an extra copy, the leader ordered, "Keep it and read it."

After taking the book, the girls hung their heads and said nothing, wishing the Red Guards would disappear.

Haughtily, the leader demanded, "Give us all your keys!"

"We have no locks on our wardrobes and boxes," Mei-Mei replied. "Father went to jail, so we're the poorest. We have nothing to lock."

"Go downstairs!" he ordered the three girls.

Little Doll was suffering from an illness at the time, and Mei-Mei asked the leader if he would let her stay resting on the bed. To her surprise, he agreed.

Mei-Mei and Lin led the way downstairs, followed by the

throng of Red Guards, who stomped, shouted, and banged with every step they took. By the time they reached the courtyard, their neighbors had crowded around.

The Red Guards set up lights and two stools. "Stand on the stools! Hands up, spies!"

The girls obeyed. The crowd formed a circle around them and gawked, some peering over others' shoulders.

"Denounce your counterrevolutionary father! Clear your name!" the Red Guards ordered.

Denounce her father? The thought repulsed Mei-Mei! She remembered when she and Lin had walked to the rice paddies outside Shanghai and discovered an onion patch. She'd uprooted an onion, carried it home, and placed it in a jar. When her father returned from work, he'd asked where it came from. When she told him, he scolded her for stealing a farmer's livelihood, gave her three renminbi, and ordered her to return the onion and pay the money to the farmer with an apology. Reluctantly she obeyed, thinking her father was paying too much for a vegetable worth only a few fen. Was the honesty she'd learned from the onion in the jar counterrevolutionary?

Another day her father had brought home a filthy street urchin he'd found rummaging in the garbage for food. Poor as they were, he served the boy all he could eat, let him bathe, and gave him a new set of clothes. When the boy left, her father had said, "We must help people more unfortunate than we!" Did an honest father with such a kind heart deserve denunciation? He'd raised her well. She determined to stand with her hands up even if all the blood in her arms ran to her feet.

"Stop corresponding with your father!"

"Admit you're spies."

Spies! Mei-Mei felt she and Lin were like orphan children, too young to be spies. Though Lin was eighteen and Mei-Mei twenty-two, neither had any connections. Accusing them of spying was ludicrous. Mei-Mei and Lin said nothing.

Someone shouted, "Cut off Second Sister's hair!"

No one acted on the idea.

"Tie a pair of old shoes around Elder Sister's neck!" Old shoes meant the sisters were promiscuous, a gross insult.

The Red Guards denounced Mei-Mei for living in such a large house. "Turn away from your decadent house! Donate it to the Liberation Army!"

Over and over they commanded the sisters to denounce their superstitious father and admit they were spies. Mei-Mei knew her sister looked to her for leadership, awaiting a signal. For hours they stood with their hands raised and said nothing.

"Look at them! The spies won't defend themselves or renounce their anti-revolutionary heritage!" the Red Guards yelled. "They're as clever as snakes to be so quiet! Very well, then, you clever little snakes don't need to say anything. Just lower your hands, and we'll know you denounce bourgeois liberalism, superstition, and your anti-party father! Just lower your hands!"

The girls had only been allowed to lower their hands long enough to adjust their glasses. Their arms were extremely tired. Mei-Mei wondered how long Lin could hold out. She couldn't let her arms down, for that would let her father down. She wanted to honor her father for her good upbringing. She allowed her glasses to slide down her nose for an excuse to adjust them. Looking over at her sister, she saw Lin's arms waver.

"All right! You won't denounce your reactionary father? Keep your hands up." Then came another threat. "If you put them down, we'll shoot you!"

The new order meant the girls could no longer adjust their glasses to rest their arms. Any movement of the arm would be hazardous. Mei-Mei noticed that a few faces in the staring crowd had tears of sympathy, but no one dared to help for fear the Red Guard would turn on them.

Mei-Mei saw her sister's hands fall slightly, and fear gripped her. A Red Guard shouted, "Second Sister has dropped her hands. We'll have to shoot her."

Words of compassion burst from Mei-Mei before she thought of the consequences. "Second Sister has had her hands up so long, she needs a rest. Please, let her drop them. Then she'll put her hands up again."

Lin's hands were already up again. The leader walked up close to the girls and stared up at them. "Whichever of you promises to be patriotic and move to the countryside—you may put down your hands!"

Mei-Mei felt so tired, she thought she couldn't bear the agony and shame another minute. Refusing to go to the countryside and work with the peasants would have ramifications she didn't want to deal with. Yet going to the countryside might make it impossible for the family ever to be reunited after her father's release. At least, the request didn't mean she was denouncing her father, and she'd be showing her loyalty to the government in an issue that wasn't moral. Her weary arms made the decision seem desirable, for she wanted the persecution to end for her sister's sake as well as for her own.

Mei-Mei extended her elbow and brushed it against Lin's. She assumed her sister understood she could promise willingness to work in the countryside, hoping they'd never actually need to leave Shanghai.

To Mei-Mei's surprise, Lin announced, "I'll cut off correspondence with my father," and lowered her arms.

Mei-Mei couldn't believe her sister's words. Why did Lin misconstrue her signal and give in? As Mei-Mei put down her arms, she said, "I'm willing to fulfill my patriotic duty and learn from the peasants in the countryside."

The Red Guards beamed victoriously. "Step down!" The girls gladly stood on solid ground. The spotlight was shut off, and the crowd dispersed. But Mei-Mei's hopes of a good night's sleep were dashed. The Red Guards grabbed the girls and marched them to the Neighborhood Committee for a trial. The girls sat opposite the young Red Guards and the elderly members of the Neighborhood Committee in the smoke-filled room.

"When you were in school, you placed pages of the Bible in your textbooks and read them when you should have been studying," the panel charged. "Confess!"

The sisters hadn't done that, but denials were called lies. They read their Bibles at home. However, even that admission might mean prison or a bullet in their heads. The girls kept silent.

"You skipped class every Saturday because of your superstition! You refused to work for the government because you were too lazy to work weekends!"

Lin had kept Sabbath regularly ever since her brother died.

Mei-Mei had refused to work for the government on Sabbath, so she hadn't been offered a job, though she'd washed her uncle's clothes and sometimes secretly sewed for her clients on Sabbath.

"Denounce your God!"

The girls kept silent.

Angrily, the Red Guards banged on the table. Denying their false accusations and ignoring their foolish questions, the tired girls feared the inquisition would never end.

After midnight, the Red Guard leader let the girls return home. Wearily, they walked through the courtyard and climbed the three flights of stairs, longing with each step for the comforts of their beds. Dismayed, they found the house in complete disarray. Clothes and bedding were strewn everywhere.

The living room gave Mei-Mei the biggest shock. "Look at the sliding door!" She pointed. "It's been sealed!"

"We've lost our second bedroom!" Lin exclaimed. "Now we must sleep with Little Doll in spite of her illness."

As Mei-Mei checked to see if her precious sewing machine was missing, she knew the Red Guards had altered their lives permanently. Soon, new tenants would live in their former bedroom. Happily, she found the sewing machine. She felt sympathy for Little Doll, who'd had to watch the destruction from her bed. "Maybe the Red Guards will leave us alone now that they know we're so poor!" she said. After tidying up the place somewhat, the girls fell into fitful sleep.

Drums, gongs, and shouts awoke the girls early the next morning. About thirty Red Guards bounded up the stairs and into the hallway, yelling, "Down with the decadent Wong sisters!" They grabbed the girls out of bed and locked them in the bathroom. "You shouldn't live in a house that uses gas for cooking. You should have a house with a coal stove."

Through the door, Mei-Mei could hear them moving the furniture down the corridor to the balcony at the top of the steps. The air became stuffy in the bathroom. Little Doll asked, "Are they leaving?"

"How are we going to get out of here if they leave?" Lin asked.

The Red Guards shouted from the balcony, "Who wants to be

a revolutionary one? Volunteer to help us throw the furniture over the banister into the courtyard. Those who refuse to cooperate are counterrevolutionaries!"

Mei-Mei answered Lin, "It's impossible for us to get out. Either we die in this bathroom or we'll be arrested as counterrevolutionaries or we volunteer to toss out our belongings." Together, the girls shouted, "We want to be revolutionary ones!"

The leader unlocked the door and led them to the balcony, where, under the supervision of the Red Guard, they threw their own furniture crashing to the ground three stories below. A great crowd gathered. Lin noticed that some neighbors had tears flowing freely down their cheeks, but no one dared say a word in the girls' defense. When all the furniture, including the bed, the wardrobe, and the sewing machine, had been cast over the banister, the girls gathered their clothes, blankets, toothbrushes, toothpaste, soap, and towels and tossed them down too. The crowd witnessed their display of loyalty. The Red Guards shouted, "Down with decadence! Down with gas stoves! Down with decadent houses!" The sisters joined in the chants. Tears blurred their vision as they realized that they'd have to move from the only home they'd ever known.

"Your counterrevolutionary father caused this," the Red Guard leader reminded them. "Go downstairs and load up!" They provided the girls with a two-wheeled pulling cart.

Tears streamed down the sisters' cheeks as they loaded the cart with their damaged bed, wardrobe, and sewing machine. Hitching themselves up as a three-girl pull team, they followed the Red Guards, dragging the heavy cart behind them, wailing with every step and wiping the tears. Where were they going? they wondered, as the Red Guard led them through the back alleys of Shanghai's slums. They longed to return to their home and live happily as they had before.

Their new quarters, narrow, very dark, with only one window, felt very hot, for on the other side of one wall were five stoves. The girls found it impossible to arrange their furniture in the tiny room, so they piled it up and squeezed their way around it.

They couldn't eat in the hot room. By nightfall, they were

famished. Mei-Mei felt certain she could not endure. A desperate idea struck her. "We still have the key. Let's move back to the old house," she suggested.

They all agreed.

Leaving their furniture behind in the hot room, they avoided the dim street lights, snuck up the three flights of stairs, and slipped undetected back into their home. They cooked a meal and slept on the floor. Awaking before dawn, Mei-Mei cooked steamed rice for breakfast. Then they slipped out of the house into the darkness and stealthily returned to the ghetto of their assigned home.

For three nights, they slept on the floor of their old home, but on the fourth night they found the lock on the door sealed. Mei-Mei said, "Let's go to the Neighborhood Committee and plead for a better home."

They didn't have to wait long after knocking on the door of the Neighborhood Committee leader in the former Japanese section. An old woman appeared and began scolding them in sharp tones. "I saw you girls from the window. Sneaking back to your old home at night! How clever you are!"

The old woman led the girls to where the elders sat. Mei-Mei pleaded, "We're willing to move, but please don't make us stay in that narrow house with no place for our furniture. It's so hot we can't eat."

"We knew decadent girls like you wouldn't want to stay there," the elders sneered, "but you must learn."

"No, please," Mei-Mei persisted. "It's not for me. I ask you for Youngest Sister, Little Doll, who is ill. If she had to live there, she'd get worse. Please, help us find another place, for Little Doll's sake."

They sounded sympathetic, discussing amongst themselves. The old woman said, "Eldest Sister is very compassionate, thinking about her Youngest Sister. We'll help you. We knew no one could live in that place. We wanted you to request a new home. Now you're here." The old woman told the girls to come with her.

The girls followed her through crowded streets to another district. They entered a maze of narrow back alleys paved with concrete in a two-story slum with plastered walls accentuated with maroon window frames and padlocked doors. The alleys were lined with layers of bicycles, baskets, tiny bamboo rattan chairs, wooden boxes, and concrete sinks. She led the girls to a dead-end alley with wooden balconies painted blood-red and corrugated metal overhanging the first-floor doors. Squashed rats and medallions of spittle dotted the cement pavement. The old woman stopped at the last door on the left and shouted.

A middle-aged tenant appeared, but she wouldn't look at the daughters of a convicted counterrevolutionary imprisoned in a hard labor camp. She allowed the old woman to lead the girls up three flights of steep, narrow ladders painted burgundy. "Have a look," the old woman said as they entered an attic. "Can you live here?"

Ducking her head through the door, Mei-Mei saw that the small attic seemed massive compared to the narrow, hot house they had rejected. She saw peeling paint, water-stained walls suggesting leaks, and a fluorescent light. One large dormer window next to the door allowed air in from the outside, and a smaller window across from it made cross ventilation. The view out each window revealed a black shingled roof with corrugated tile. The boards in the floor squeaked as they sank slightly under her weight. A quick mental calculation suggested that, small though the attic was, Mei-Mei and her sisters could find space to arrange the furniture. Given the alternative, Mei-Mei thanked the old woman for her "fine choice" and announced, "We can live here."

After leaving the attic, the old woman led them out of the maze, and they parted. Mei-Mei wondered how they would transport their furniture from the hot house to the attic. No one dared assist the daughters of a counterrevolutionary, so the Wong sisters carried everything themselves, loading it on a cart and dragging it through the slum to their attic home. The middle-aged woman who functioned as a landlady—though China officially had no landlord class after liberation—offered the girls nothing but reproof, forcing them to move in and arrange their room by their own feeble strength.

They struggled with the furniture as they lifted and twisted it up the three narrow ladders, fearing they might lose their grip and fall. With difficulty, they coaxed every piece through the little door. Wearily, Mei-Mei shoved a bed next to the door and put the sewing machine under the large window. A chair and the wardrobe fit between the bed and the small window. Relaxing on the bed, Mei-Mei felt sorry that the house would be too small to share comfortably with her father after he was set free. However, they were still in Shanghai and could welcome him after his release. But where could they cook except in the alley?

Their stomachs complained, so Lin and Mei-Mei climbed down the ladders to make a coal fire on the street outside the landlord's home. The two sisters placed wastepaper and chips of wood into a stove and struck a match, then placed coal inside and fanned the flames. But when the stove was hot enough to cook on, neighborhood children taunted them, calling them counterrevolutionary scum and poking sticks into the stove to knock out the coals. Tired and frustrated, Lin cried and dashed upstairs. Mei-Mei stayed and tried again.

After days of conflict with the neighbor children, Mei-Mei decided the naughty children should be chastised. Under the Cultural Revolution, their mothers seemed fearful to teach them proper manners. She determined that since she was already disgraced through her father's imprisonment, she had nothing to lose. Picking up one little boy, she glared at him, then dropped him. When he got up, all the children ran away.

None of them bothered the sisters again.

Chapter 27

FIVE-FLOWER KNOT AND A BUCKET

For several years, the guards who knew Mr. Wong realized that they couldn't change his beliefs, so they left him unmolested to serve his time. This made it possible for him to talk freely with trusted prisoners about his Friend Jesus. However, in 1968, with the renewed vigor of the Cultural Revolution, new guards were assigned to the hard labor camp who were determined to reeducate him.

One day in 1968 a guard entered his niche and called out his name gruffly. "Mr. Wong, follow me!"

Mr. Wong followed the guard to another niche in the cave. "Criminal Lin!" he shouted. "Come here."

A prisoner whom Mr. Wong recognized stood to his feet and came toward the guard.

The guard then turned back to Mr. Wong. "Criminal Wong!" he snapped, "do you know why you are in prison?"

Mr. Wong had lost track of how many times he had heard that question. "Yes," he said.

"Why?"

"Because I believe in the Real God."

"You must glorify our Great Helmsman, Chairman Mao! You can't continue breaking our laws without us knowing." Turning to the other inmate, he demanded, "Criminal Lin! Tell me again what Criminal Wong told you on the way to town."

"On our day off," Inmate Lin began, "Old Wong and I were walking along the road into town, when he spoke against the Great Helmsman, our great leader, Chairman Mao Tse-tung.

Long live Chairman Mao!"

"Repeat what he said."

Inmate Lin looked at Mr. Wong. "He said, 'If Chairman Mao wants me to die and God wants me to live, I will live; if God wants me to die and Chairman Mao wants me to live, I will die.'"

"You see, Criminal Wong, we watch everything you do and hear all you say." The guard looked condescendingly at him. "Will you stop talking this bourgeois liberalistic nonsense? Religion is the opiate of the people."

The guard took Mr. Wong out of the niche into the center of the cave and ordered all prisoners to join them. The prisoners shouted, "This man said his God is stronger than Chairman Mao! He must be punished!"

The strongest of the prisoners, an inmate named Sun Chiyee, tied Mr. Wong's hands behind his back, then lifted them upward until Mr. Wong had to bend his back slightly to ease the pain. Then he wrapped the rope around Mr. Wong's neck and wound it back down to his hands just tight enough that it wouldn't choke him if he stood straight, but standing straight hurt his arms. Inmate Sun continued winding the rope over Mr. Wong's shoulder and around his waist and back to his hands. When he had completed his task, the ropes looked like a star or flower in front. Admiring his handiwork, Sun Chiyee declared, "My Five-Flower Tie is the perfect knot. There is no way you can untie it without breaking your arms or choking to death. Now, Criminal Wong, give up your God!"

A guard praised Sun Chiyee's work. "For tying the Five-Flower Knot, he'll receive merit. His time in prison is reduced! Who else wants merit?"

An extremely cruel persecutor, a prisoner named Tan Taiyang, stepped forward. Mr. Wong recalled that this man had nearly beaten his own son to death to gain a few prison merits. Tan Taiyang had a bucket full of water and a rope. After tying the bucket around Mr. Wong's neck, Inmate Tan grabbed a heavy whetstone and dropped it into the bucket, jolting Mr. Wong's head forward. This caused him to gasp for air and raise his head, which hurt his arms. Before Mr. Wong could readjust his position, Tan Taiyang slapped his face three times and shouted, "Confess!"

Mr. Wong remembered how Jesus, his Friend, when persecuted at His trial in Herod's palace, remained silent, so he said nothing. His outer body felt strained, skewed, and torn, but inside he was filled with joy.

Hoping to gain more merit, the judas stepped forward and slapped Mr. Wong's face over and over again, saying, "Give up your God, and all your troubles will be over!" Then the three hundred prisoners lined up, and, one by one, took turns slapping Mr. Wong's face and yelling, "Are you going to repent or not?"

The slapping and taunting continued for the entire work period. The monotonous words sounded to Mr. Wong like so much noise. His face became swollen and bloody. The bucket hanging from his neck and the Five-Flower Knot made it impossible to stand erect without choking. Any effort to straighten his shoulders pulled his arms up his back toward his neck, forcing him to lower his neck to alleviate the pain in his arms and thus tighten the rope around his neck. Each time another hand slapped him, he could hardly keep his balance and inhale.

The pain in his arms, neck, and face screamed at him to confess and give up his God. Then words from Jesus rang in his mind, "Confess Me, and I will confess you before God; deny Me, and sadly, I will also deny you." How could he deny his Friend Jesus, who had died that he, Mr. Wong, might live? He desired eternal life, not just a few more years in China. The prophet Isaiah, who was sawed in two by King Menasseh, promised that "no weapon formed against you will prosper" (Isaiah 54:17). Mr. Wong didn't believe his ragged, torn body would never die, but if the persecutors killed him, he knew that one day the Real God would tear down the gates of hell and prevail against all his enemies. From evidence in the Bible and from Ellen G. White's writings, he was convinced that a war between good and evil was raging and that only God could save him from death. If he was on God's side in the battle against evil, he would live again at the second coming of his Friend Jesus. Despite the pain, he refused to recant his belief in God.

When the workday came to an end, the inquisition party left Mr. Wong standing. The next day the ritual resumed. And the next. And the next. The prisoners intensified the stress. The pain grew worse. His arms felt like lead behind his back, and his hunched back hurt his spine. The rope around his neck compressed his voice box. It was tight around his shoulders, waist, and hands, pinching his circulation and breathing. His body stank from the combination of his own sweat, blood, urine, and dung. His anguish grew darker and deeper. Exhausted from lack of sleep, he ached to sit down or lie down so his feet could enjoy a moment's respite.

The prisoners slapped his face until his skin puffed over his eyes and he could no longer see them. The scabs from previous days reopened, and blood, mixed with dirt and sweat, oozed out.

"Confess!" the prisoners yelled. "Write out a confession in a self-criticism and live!" "Repeat! Repeat!" they urged.

Mr. Wong's body urged him to take the easy way, but his inner man remembered the cold night when Lee Man Kai had tied him up and left him to die. Mr. Wong recalled how the knot had been miraculously loosened and later tightened. Not all miracle stories happened in the Bible. The Real God could work a miracle for him again if He so desired. The memory gave him strength to remain loyal to Jesus. For his Friend's sake, he could not recant. Perhaps tomorrow the pain would be unbearable, but not today. When they ordered him to confess, he replied No.

Each day after that, he felt sure that tomorrow he might have to surrender, but not today. By putting off the confession to the next day, he could resist the pain another day. After seventeen days of torture, Mr. Wong's inner man grew impatient. He wanted the prisoners to know that their work was futile. Could he force his tormentors to stop persecuting him?

As the days and nights of torment dragged on, Mr. Wong, a lover of words, had uttered hardly a sound.

When the slaps and repeated cries of "Confess!" came on the seventeenth day, Mr. Wong opened his parched and bleeding lips to say, "You don't understand!" Silence reigned momentarily. "My answer is No! Even if Chairman Mao himself were standing here asking me to recant and deny my God, I'd still say No!

I can't deny my Friend Jesus!"

Rather than dampening the enthusiasm of his persecutors as he had expected, the words fired them up. The familiar voice of Sun Chiyee screamed, "Confess! Confess! Confess!" Inmate Sun angrily grabbed Mr. Wong's arms, tied behind his back, and lifted them over his head and brought them down to his waist in front, ripping the tendons in his shoulders and breaking both arms. Tears welled up in Mr. Wong's eyes, stinging as they coursed down his swollen and bloodied cheeks. Mr. Wong prayed to his Friend for help to endure.

"It's enough!" the supervising guard ordered. "Stop! If we kill Criminal Wong, we can't help him develop."

"Let me untie him!" Mr. Wong heard Inmate Sun request. He felt Sun's robust arms untying the knot and lifting him off the ground. Pain from his torn ligaments caused more tears. He sensed himself being carried out of the burrow and into the gusty wind above ground on the prison compound. Mr. Sun loosened his grasp, and Mr. Wong felt himself falling, landing hard on his broken arms.

Mr. Wong lay in a heap on the ground within the prison walls. Bruised, bloodied, and blind, his arms broken, he couldn't grope his way back to his niche in the burrow. In his misery he moaned that he'd be better off dead than alive, but his inner soul praised God he had survived and won another victory these past seventeen days as a witness to the prisoners.

A while later he heard footsteps approaching. Someone bent over him, attempting to roll him over. When a hand touched his shoulder, pain struck him. "Relax, Criminal Wong." He recognized the accent of the guard who had organized the prisoners to persecute him. "I'm here to help you."

Mr. Wong knew his soothing voice was insincere.

"They would have killed you, but I saved your life, Criminal Wong, so listen to what I say. Please, don't resist liberation."

Mr. Wong said nothing.

"You're badly hurt. Your face is swollen and covered with scabs. It appears as if Criminal Sun broke your arms. I'll make sure he's punished for that. I'll take you to a doctor."

"Please, don't take me to a doctor," Mr. Wong urged. "Take

me to my bed."

"Criminal Wong, stubbornness has become a habit for you that takes you beyond reason. Granted, your injuries are justified under the circumstances, but now you need your benign government's help."

Mr. Wong knew that the man offering aid was responsible for his injuries.

"I don't need to see a doctor," Mr. Wong insisted. "Jesus, my Friend, the Son of the Real God, will heal my arms."

The guard laughed cynically. He began lifting Mr. Wong, careful not to touch his shoulders. Standing on his swollen feet, he felt the guard gently guide his steps. "Take me to my bed," Mr. Wong persisted.

"You're right," the guard said kindly. "You've had a hard time, and you need rest."

Mr. Wong felt himself being guided down into the cave, into his niche. He heard the guard light a candle. Ever so gently, he assisted Mr. Wong onto the floor and pulled the blanket over him. "After you're rested up, I'll take you to a doctor." The niche became silent, so Mr. Wong assumed that the guard had left.

Alone with his thoughts, Mr. Wong remembered an experience in the Shanghai prison. While awaiting trial, he had contracted a urinary tract infection that had blocked his system entirely. After weeks of unsuccessful treatment from the prison doctor, he'd told Jesus, his Friend, of the doctor's failure and his discomfort. Immediately, the infection had cleared. Remembering that miracle, he prayed again. "My Friend Jesus, I don't want to see the doctor. The guards will use his aid to pressure me to deny You. I believe You can perform a miracle for me, because Your reputation is at stake. They say I stubbornly cling to superstition. Please heal my arms and face to prove to both prisoners and jailers that You are the Real God. Show the government that true Christians need no liberation."

No tingles shot through his spine. The pain persisted, but he rested in faith, assured of eventual healing. All was dark. He couldn't open his eyes. Easing his arms into a comfortable position, he waited. When the guard returned, offering to take him to a doctor, Mr. Wong refused. "The Real God will heal me. Wait, and you will see."

The guard laughed in disbelief. "All right, but I'll be back. When you can no longer tolerate the pain, tell me. Then we'll visit the doctor."

Mr. Wong heard the guard walk away. He slept uncomfortably, but when he awakened, he knew the pain had decreased slightly, which gave him hope. He could see the candle; and when the guard returned, Mr. Wong could make out some of the man's facial features. He again refused to accompany the guard to the doctor.

He lay in bed the whole day, while everyone around him worked and ate. During the whole time, he prayed for a miracle. "My Friend Jesus, I know the doctor can cure me, but I don't want the government to claim the credit, when You really did it." By the end of the day, he could move his arms with little pain.

"I wish you could see your face, Old Wong," one of his roommates exclaimed when he returned from his shift. "Your God must be with you, because the swelling is down to the point where I can see your eyes, and your scabs are flaking off, revealing healthy skin as smooth as a baby's."

When the guard came again, Mr. Wong smiled. "I can see you now."

"Of course, your swelling is down! That's natural—but your arms are broken!"

Mr. Wong again refused to see a doctor.

When the guard showed up the third day, he brought an inmate-physician. Mr. Wong smiled. "I don't need a doctor. My arms don't hurt. My Friend Jesus healed me, just as I said. I told you my God is the Real God!"

Mr. Wong rejoiced inwardly as the doctor examined him, noting that the swelling was down and the scabs had flaked off. Thanking God for the miracle, Mr. Wong moved his arms freely, as if his shoulders had never been dislocated or his arms broken. In amazement, the doctor exclaimed, "I saw your injuries." Mumbling under his breath, he added, "I don't know how to explain it!"

"Good! Glad you're in good health, Criminal Wong!" the guard said, but his voice carried a note of utter astonishment, and his words sounded garbled. "Tomorrow you can go back to work!"

Chapter 28

SELF-CRITICISM AND THE COUNTERREVOLUTIONARY HAT

One day in July 1979, the guards summoned all the prisoners into the center of the burrow. Instead of the routine roll call they expected, though, the chief guard made a surprising announcement.

"The Gang of Four's terrible reign was overthrown in the 'October coup,'" he said, "and Chairman Hua Guofeng is searching out radical elements. Premier Deng Xiaoping himself suffered twice during the ten wasted years of the Cultural Revolution because he was falsely accused of being a 'capitalist roader' opposed to Mao's teachings. Premier Deng's son was thrown from a window and paralyzed in a raid during the catastrophic years of the Cultural Revolution. Premier Deng realizes many people were incarcerated unjustly by the Gang of Four. He wants reforms to advance New China toward the Four Modernizations."

As he listened, Mr. Wong wondered why the Gang of Four and the Cultural Revolution were being made the scapegoats for Chairman Mao's policies. He had been imprisoned eight years before the Cultural Revolution and eighteen years before the Gang of Four came into power.

"Deng wants to reform the prisons," the guard continued, "and remove the 'counterrevolutionary hat' from everyone incarcerated unjustly." Mr. Wong knew that a "counterrevolutionary hat" was a euphemism for a suspected person's status in his official record. Removal of such a euphemism required compliance with the Party and exoneration, the twin goals of every prisoner.

"In support of those reforms," the guard concluded, "I want

the nineteen criminals from the original five thousand to form a struggle session. Guards, organize the prisoners into a circle, and have them criticize one another!"

At once, the prisoners began accusing each other of breaking China's regulations and talking against the government, but Mr. Wong refused to criticize anyone. Most prisoners had no basis for what they said.

When required to speak, Mr. Wong confessed, "I'm a true Christian who believes my Friend Jesus is the Saviour who died on Calvary to give us immortality in the next life, providing we follow Him and live by His Ten Regulations. The signs of the times indicate He is returning soon to take His own to heaven."

"You must give up such superstition, Old Wong, if you ever want your counterrevolutionary hat removed!" yelled some prisoners.

"The Chinese constitution guarantees freedom of religion, so I'm glad to hear about reforms," Mr. Wong replied. "We Christians wait patiently to be reinstated. With a reform-minded government in power, I hope to return to Shanghai soon!"

Some laughed. "You're in prison. The government wouldn't have sentenced an innocent man. Confess!"

"I confess I was a deacon in the Seventh-day Adventist church and worshiped the Real God every Sabbath," Mr. Wong answered. "My duties included ushering people to their seats and taking up the tithes and offerings."

Another prisoner, when called to confess, stood up and protested angrily, "I won't confess to lies! Down with New China! Long live Chiang Kai-shek and the capitalist road in Taiwan!" He yelled other counterrevolutionary slogans about the Kuomintang.

The guards shouted, "Kneel! Raise your hands!"

Panicking, the prisoner bolted for the exit, but instantly a shot rang out, and he slumped to the ground. A guard kicked his body to be certain he was dead.

The struggle session stopped. Breaking the silence, the chief guard arose. "Go to your niches, and write self-criticisms. Tell us everything. This is your last chance to confess."

Mr. Wong had written his "last confession" repeatedly. The

result had added months to his prison term for what his jailers called stubbornness. Instead of seeking the government's rewards or merits, he desired God's rewards.

"Think seriously, frankly, and honestly," the chief guard counseled. "The government will make one final decision. If your self-criticism is satisfactory, Deng Xiaoping will release you. If not, you will be shot." The guards handed out paper to the prisoners, who went to their niches. Mr. Wong did not write an ordinary self-criticism. He did not detail his life, confess his crimes to the government, or extol reeducation. He did not mention his unworthiness nor suggest to the Party a suitable punishment to complete his reeducation that would convert him to the socialist road. Instead, in eleven points, he explained true Christianity and his involvement in the church, making it clear that his relationship with the Real God superseded his obeying New China's laws.

Having finished his confession, he delivered it to a guard, hoping and praying for the best.

As Mr. Wong sat cross-legged on his blanket reading his medical book, a guard entered his niche and waved his confession in the air. "Criminal Wong, it's not satisfactory! We have a regulation against the superstition of prayer. You must tell the government whether you will continue to pray after you're released."

"Prayer is the only means I have to communicate with the Real God." Mr. Wong set down his medical book.

"You failed to mention prayer in your confession. If you want your counterrevolutionary hat removed, Criminal Wong, write a self-criticism about prayer as a supplement to your final confession. I want it tonight."

Handing him a sheet of paper, the guard asked, "Why do you pray?"

"As long as a true Christian is alive, he will pray." Mr. Wong smiled, eager to witness. "I love to talk to my Friend Jesus. True Christians pray before doing anything, but only to the Real God, never to any person or object. We pray, with or without sound, every day before eating and sleeping."

"Prayer is an opiate," the guard retorted. "Come with me."

Mr. Wong followed the guard out of the burrow and past the

sentry's mound in the center of the compound. Outside the prison walls, where no one but the guard could hear, Mr. Wong explained, "Daniel prayed three times a day in Babylon. The angry king ordered that anyone praying to God would be thrown into a lions' den. Daniel still prayed and was thrown to hungry lions, but the Real God shut their mouths." The two walked past an adobe-walled corral. Inside, a prison unit was picking up chunks of sheep and goat dung with their hands and placing it in baskets.

Mr. Wong continued, "The Old and New Testaments tell how Joshua's army needed more time in battle to defeat the enemy. So Joshua prayed, asking the Real God to cause the sun to stay in the sky for an extra day, enabling Joshua to kill all his enemies. When the battle was over, the sun sank."

"Surely, Criminal Wong, you don't believe such fables."

Mr. Wong regretted that the guard had known him only a short time and was thus unaware of how God had helped him in prison. "In 1964, I was pulled out from my unit because I refused to work on Sabbath. The prisoners tied me up and threw me to the ground. The guards threatened to shoot me, but I knelt and prayed. When the leader asked why I was praying, I told him, 'Prayer is food for the soul. I don't care about my life, because life is so short on this earth. I'll die sooner or later, but in heaven I will live forever.' Impressed, the guard stood me up and said he wouldn't shoot me. So my prayer was answered. Whatever circumstances or persecutions, nothing can stop a true Christian from praying to the Real God."

"Your experience had nothing to do with your God, Criminal Wong," the guard retorted; "rather, it indicates the kindness of your government. Which reminds me that you forgot to tell the Party whether you would refuse to work on Saturday if you are released. To remove your counterrevolutionary hat, you must add that to your supplement tonight."

"The government knows I'm a hard worker," Mr. Wong replied as the two joined a work team in the Tibetan corral. The prisoners had emptied their baskets of dung over the barley field and were returning to refill them. "I work honestly for the government," Mr. Wong continued, "and I'm willing to do anything. The Testaments teach that from the sweat on your face you shall eat rice, but it also says I should work six days and rest on Sabbath."

The guard watched the prisoners picking up the dung. "But, Criminal Wong, you can gain rewards if you alter your thinking."

"I've told every leader in Tsinghai's labor camp that I don't want merit." Mr. Wong smiled. "Through the years, I've seen my name on the list offering me rewards, but I refuse to earn merit if I have to go against one of the Ten Regulations found in Exodus 20. I promise to work hard for the government six days a week, but I'll continue celebrating my friendship with Jesus every Sabbath after I'm released."

"One last thing you forgot to mention, Criminal Wong," the guard advised. "Answer this question in your last supplement: Will you cling to your superstitious insistence of eating vegetarian food?"

"I appreciate the government's kindness to serve me vegetarian food." Mr. Wong wondered if the guard's inquiries were sincere. "When I requested food without lard, the government didn't understand at first, but because I worked hard, it decided to take care of my body, not my belief. I am vegetarian for health reasons, which has helped me to survive my prison term."

The work team had filled their baskets again and headed for the fields. Mr. Wong and the guard followed them. "I hope you'll rethink your stubborn ideas and embrace New China, for we live in a new day now."

"I want to request travel papers to visit my daughters in Shanghai," Mr. Wong said.

"Maybe permission cannot be granted. If so, you have no way; but China is reforming, Criminal Wong, and there's no turning back. Maybe the patience of the Christians will be rewarded someday. I'll accept your request when you give me the supplement to your self-criticism."

The guard left, and the team leader issued Mr. Wong a basket. Joining the other workers, he filled his basket with dung. When they had finished for the day, he returned to his niche and worked on his supplement, writing the same ideas he had expressed to the guard. He delivered it, along with his request for travel papers to Shanghai.

While chewing his steamed rolls and barley the next day, the guard who had demanded his self-criticism entered the cave and presented him with some slips of paper. "Criminal Wong, here are your travel papers. However, the government has decided it cannot provide for your transportation. You'll have to pay for that yourself. I have permission to release you for a holiday from Tsinghai Province, but you must return in one month."

How impossible to return in a month, Mr. Wong thought. *With no transportation and no money, I'll have to walk or ask lorry drivers for lifts*. Opening the document, he found, to his dismay, that his "counterrevolutionary hat" had not been removed. If he wanted a ride, he must show his papers to the driver, who would surely reject him when he saw that he still had a "counterrevolutionary hat."

"You're a very lucky man, Criminal Wong!" The guard interrupted Mr. Wong's reverie as he passed out slips of paper to four other prisoners. "You came to Tsinghai from Shanghai with 1,500 prisoners, and, over the last twenty years, 3,500 other prisoners have also come here from Shanghai. Today, eighteen of those five thousand are left, and only five of them were chosen for release. You are one of those five! Each of them requested travel papers to visit their families. All were denied a holiday except for you. I don't know why you are so lucky!"

Mr. Wong thought that luck had nothing to do with it. Despite the problems he still faced, he considered his travel papers a miracle.

"Maybe your God was with you, Criminal Wong."

Knowing that he must leave very soon, or he would never complete his journey, Mr. Wong immediately packed up his meager belongings. But he wanted his daughters to understand what he had experienced in prison. He wanted them to read about it before he arrived. He didn't feel it proper to talk about his suffering while they were together, for he wanted their reunion to be a joyous time. So he wrote a poem with seven characters to a line, so arranged that every line had the same rhythm.

Folding up the poem, he placed it in an envelope. Contrary to prison regulations, he stuck it in the mailbox when no one was looking. Prisoners were forbidden to post letters without first giving them to the wardens for approval, but he knew that they would reject his poem on two accounts: its message and its length, for it exceeded the maximum number of characters. Prisoners were expected to write that "all was well" and "everyone was fine." The guards always scolded prisoners when they discovered an unapproved letter. He knew he had succeeded in three previous attempts, for he hadn't been scolded.

The mail carrier, who arrived monthly, was due any minute. Mr. Wong waited for him as inconspicuously as possible. The postal carrier immediately noticed Mr. Wong's letter. Since none of the prison staff was in sight, he asked, "Has this letter been approved?"

The mail carrier had once been a prisoner in the labor camp, and Mr. Wong knew him. "Please, comrade, send it for me just this once," Mr. Wong begged. "I've been granted a month's holiday, and I want my daughters to get a special letter before I come."

"I'll be risking a lot, Old Wong."

"I'm soon to be released, Comrade," Mr. Wong said, "so I won't be asking this favor again. Please; it's important!"

The postal carrier smiled and slipped the letter into his bag.

With no money for his trip to Shanghai other than what he'd managed to save from a meager stipend the government paid for prisoners to buy necessities, Mr. Wong set out on foot, knowing everything hinged on hitching a ride. Ashamed of his "counterrevolutionary hat," he grew shy. Even though the proof of his hated "hat" was only written on a paper in his pocket, Mr. Wong feared that everyone knew he was a former inmate. Freedom had not yet given him confidence.

Walking down the dusty road, he reached a service station where the big blue trucks that traveled the roads stopped to refuel. Anyone, especially any driver, could ask, "Show me your identity and travel papers," and he would be required to oblige. Once the driver saw on his papers his "counterrevolutionary hat," he would probably be denied a ride.

Prayerfully, Mr. Wong read the faces of drivers and passengers. He felt attracted to a young man standing alone near one blue truck. Though he feared a rebuff, faith propelled him to action. Approaching timidly, Mr. Wong asked, "Where are you going?"

"We're heading east."

"I'm going to Shanghai." Mr. Wong smiled. "Could I ride with you?"

"Sure," the young man answered, "but I'm not the driver." He looked over his shoulder and pointed out a short, stocky middle-aged man. "That's the driver. If he says it's all right, you can ride with us."

With another prayer, Mr. Wong asked, "Can you ask him for me?"

The young man agreed.

Feeling relieved that he hadn't asked for his identity and travel papers, Mr. Wong dared to hope that the driver wouldn't either. Staying with his new friend, he watched as the passengers reassembled. Then the young man walked to the driver and said, "This man asked if he could ride with us. I said it was your decision."

The driver turned to Mr. Wong with stern eyes and demanded, "Show me your papers!"

Hearing the dreaded words, Mr. Wong panicked but remained outwardly calm. As nonchalantly as possible, he handed over the papers. The driver read some of the characters several times. Then he looked Mr. Wong up and down, studying his face thoughtfully. After what seemed a lifetime, he handed the papers back and grunted, "You look like an honest man. Come along!"

As he climbed onto the back of the truck, Mr. Wong hoped that when he arrived in Shanghai, the loss of his "counterrevolutionary hat" and his subsequent reinstatement would be granted as easily.

EPILOGUE

During the years he spent at the hard labor camp, Mr. Wong's daughters all grew up and married. Conditions had eased a great deal by the time he arrived back in Shanghai. His daughters and their husbands all had good homes. Mei-Mei and Lin each had a little girl, making Mr. Wong twice a grandfather. Shortly after his arrival in Shanghai, Mei-Mei wrote to the labor camp where her father had been imprisoned, requesting permission for him to stay in Shanghai longer. The request was granted, and eventually he was able to clear his name and receive permission for permanent residence in Shanghai. He never returned to the hard labor camp.

Much freedom of religion has returned to China. Neither his daughters nor their husbands have Sabbath problems with their work, and they worship in their churches without fear of persecution. Mr. Wong is grateful for these changes, which make today's China a truly New China.